Conventional Coercion Across the Spectrum of Operations

The Utility of U.S. Military
Forces in the Emerging
Security Environment

David E. Johnson
Karl P. Mueller
William H. Taft, V

Prepared for the
United States Army

Arroyo Center

RAND

The research described in this report was sponsored by the United States Army under Contract No. DASW01-01-C-0003.

Library of Congress Cataloging-in-Publication Data

Johnson, David E., 1950 Oct. 10–
    Conventional coercion across the spectrum of operations : the utility of U.S. military forces in the emerging security environment / David E. Johnson, Karl P. Mueller, William H. Taft V.
      p. cm.
    "MR-1494."
    Includes bibliographical references.
    ISBN 0-8330-3220-8
    1. United States—Military policy. 2. United States—Armed Forces. 3. World politics—21st century. 4. National security—United States. I. Mueller, Karl P. II. Taft, William H., V. III. Title.

UA23 .J57 2002
327.1' 17'0973—dc21

2002068218

RAND is a nonprofit institution that helps improve policy and decisionmaking through research and analysis. RAND® is a registered trademark. RAND's publications do not necessarily reflect the opinions or policies of its research sponsors.

Published 2002 by RAND
1700 Main Street, P.O. Box 2138, Santa Monica, CA 90407-2138
1200 South Hayes Street, Arlington, VA 22202-5050
201 North Craig Street, Suite 202, Pittsburgh, PA 15213-1516
RAND URL: http://www.rand.org/
To order RAND documents or to obtain additional information, contact Distribution Services: Telephone: (310) 451-7002;
Fax: (310) 451-6915; Email: order@rand.org

This study presents the results of research conducted as part of an Arroyo Center project on structuring U.S. combat capabilities for early conflict termination. The purpose of the overall project was to define the force capabilities and conditions best suited to deter a potential enemy or lead to his early defeat. The focus of the research reported here was on conventional deterrence in the post–Cold War era. The research was sponsored by the Director of Strategy, Plans, and Policy, Deputy Chief of Staff for Operations (DCSOPS), U.S. Army.

This report is intended to provide an introduction to the coercive use of conventional military power for military and civilian professionals involved in the practical application of such power.

The research was conducted in the Strategy, Doctrine, and Resources Program of the Arroyo Center. The Arroyo Center is a federally funded research and development center sponsored by the United States Army.

For more information on RAND Arroyo Center, contact the Director
of Operations (telephone 310-393-0411, extension 6500; FAX 310-
451-6952; e-mail donnab@rand.org), or visit the Arroyo Center's Web
site at http://www.rand.org/ard/.

CONTENTS

FIGURES AND TABLES

Figures

Tables

The United States, despite its unrivaled political and military power in the post–Cold War era, faces an international security environment inherently more ambiguous and potentially less stable than at any time since the end of World War II. Furthermore, because of the inherent complexity of the situation—coupled with the absence of the principal organizing intellectual construct for the uses of national power that guided the containment of the Soviet Union during the Cold War—the United States has found itself largely in a reactive posture, forced to deal with each challenge on a case-by-case basis and often with only brief warning. One of the central questions facing policymakers engaged in formulating national security policy is that of crafting strategies—and shaping the military forces to execute the strategies—to deter future conflict.

This report is intended to provide an introduction to the coercive use of conventional military power for military and civilian professionals involved in the practical application of such power. It focuses on conventional coercion, employing two approaches in the assessment of which force capabilities and conditions are most likely to coerce a potential enemy or lead to his early defeat. First, we reviewed the literature on coercion to identify relevant theory, developed working definitions, and located conflict databases and assessed their utility. Although we provide definitions for coercion that include all the elements of national power (diplomatic, economic, informational, and military), we concentrate on the utility of military power as a coercive instrument in deterrence and compellence—and if coercion fails, conflict termination. Second, we selected and analyzed cases (both U.S. and foreign, successes and failures) that would provide insights into conventional coercion across the spectrum of military operations. The case analysis focused on the following:

- Assessing what form(s) of coercion were involved.
- Distilling insights about why the coercion was successful or unsuccessful.
- Determining the force packages employed in the cases and which of their capabilities were most effective.
- Deriving insights from the cases that should be relevant in the future.

For purposes of sorting the cases, we used four categories: stability and support operations, smaller-scale contingencies, major theater wars, and strikes and raids.

We also developed a theoretical framework in an effort to answer the following question: What does it take to coerce? We postulate that to answer this question one must make two fundamental assessments. The first assessment is qualitative: an analysis of the adversary's deterrence/compellence threshold vis-à-vis the issue at stake (the context). The second is largely quantitative: an assessment of the capabilities possessed by the adversary. From this appreciation, a net assessment can be conducted to determine the adversary's strengths and weaknesses and what will likely be required to coerce or defeat him. In short, one must understand the adversary's will and capabilities to determine the resources and means necessary to coerce him and, if coercion fails, to force him to meet your demands.

In the final chapter of the report, we provide a matrix that combines our theoretical coercion framework with the cases we analyzed. Using this construct, we gleaned insights about the degree of effort and the force mixes required at different points along the spectrum of operations to coerce the adversaries analyzed in the cases. Two other sets of insights are also presented. First, we provide a table that compares the positive attributes and the potential liabilities of ground (Army and Marine Corps), air, and naval forces from the perspective of their utility as coercive instruments. Second, we discuss the following insights specifically regarding the use of ground forces in coercion strategies or interventions:

- At the lower end of the spectrum of operations, early arriving and capable ground forces often have high value. Indeed, in stability and support operations (where population control is essential— e.g., KFOR in Kosovo) and strikes (where the objective is to change a regime that has marginal capabilities—e.g., Operation Just Cause in Panama), ground forces offer the most, and often the only, effective military option.

- At the higher end of the spectrum (where U.S. ground forces are not already present), early arriving ground forces demonstrate U.S. commitment, both to friends and foes, and they potentially deny the aggressor the prospect of an easy victory—but with some risk. Unless ground forces are operating in an environment of air superiority, and with substantial joint presence to compensate for the lack of mass of the initial ground force vis-à-vis the adversary, they can be at great risk (e.g., Task Force Smith during the Korean War). Therefore, some form of joint or coalition support must be available in-theater in situations where the adversary has significant capabilities in case friendly ground forces need to be built up. In short, ground tripwires must have substantial joint capability behind them if they are to be militarily as well as politically significant.

- Modest in-place U.S. ground forces (e.g., Korea, Southwest Asia, Bosnia, Kosovo), backed up by joint and coalition capabilities, have a significant deterrent value and provide a regional stabilizing effect. They also deny the adversary the prospect of an easy victory and send a clear signal of U.S. commitment. Finally, they provide a base around which follow-on U.S. forces can form.

- Historical examples that might support the hypothesis that an early arriving ground force can preclude aggression by an adversary are ambiguous, although the threat of an imminent airborne assault did result in Raul Cedras leaving power in Haiti in 1994. This is particularly true in the case of an adversary that has significant military capabilities. Again, what early arriving ground forces primarily demonstrate is U.S. resolve: They are the harbinger of a much larger, overwhelming follow-on force (e.g., Operation Desert Shield), and thus their specific military capabilities are less important than their political significance.

- Unsuccessful interventions (e.g., Vietnam, Somalia) can have lasting effects beyond the realm of military operations in that they can negatively affect U.S. political will, reduce the credibility of U.S. military deterrence abroad, and raise potential adversaries' perceptions of the contestability of U.S. power.

- Deterrence/intervention successes that do not remove the preconditions that caused the conflict can lead to long-term commitments to ongoing coercive regimes (e.g., Korea, Southwest Asia).

As the United States develops national security and national military strategies for the future security environment, the challenges are complex. Although the more familiar threat of cross-border, interstate aggression is still a possibility that must be deterred in some regions, new and different security problems must be addressed in the future. Internal wars that have external dimensions because of their threats to U.S. interests, their humanitarian dimensions (including genocide), and their effect on U.S. public opinion may again require action. Furthermore, the nature of future threats, particularly with the proliferation of weapons of mass destruction and major international terrorism, will require new approaches to deterrence, particularly in the realm of homeland security. This report, however, shows that the essential nature of devising effective coercive strategies has not changed. One must understand not only an adversary's capabilities and the threshold that must be reached to coerce him, but also effectively communicate to him that you have both the will and the capability to prevail.

ACKNOWLEDGMENTS

The authors gratefully acknowledge the assistance of the following colleagues at RAND who contributed to this research: David Chu, Rick Brennan, Paul Davis, John Gordon, Steve Hosmer, Antoine Jaureguiberry, David Kassing, Tom McNaugher, Walt Perry, Bruce Pirnie, Ted Warner, and Jay Wise. We also express our appreciation to Davis Bobrow and Jim Quinlivan for their thorough and thoughtful reviews of an earlier version of this study. The insights and contributions of all these individuals added immeasurably to the final product.

ABBREVIATIONS

AB	Air base
AEF	Air Expeditionary Force
AFB	Air Force base
CANG	California National Guard
CONUS	Continental United States
DMZ	Demilitarized zone
DPRK	Democratic People's Republic of Korea
FDO	Flexible deterrent options
FLN	Force Liberation Nationale (Algeria)
IFOR	Implementation Force (Bosnia)
JTF-LA	Joint Task Force–Los Angeles
JTF-SWA	Joint Task Force–Southwest Asia
KFOR	Kosovo Force
LAPD	Los Angeles Police Department
MEU	Marine Expeditionary Unit
MFO	Multinational Force and Observers
MTW	Major theater war
NATO	North Atlantic Treaty Organization
NEO	Noncombatant evacuation operation
OAS	Organization of American States

PDF	Panamanian Defense Forces
ROK	Republic of Korea
SASO	Stability and support operations
SCA	Support to civil authorities
SFOR	Stabilization Force (Bosnia)
SSC	Smaller-scale contingency
UN	United Nations
UNC	UN Command
UNITAF	Operation Restore Hope
UNOSOM I	Operation Provide Relief
UNOSOM II	Operation Continue Hope
UNPREDEP	UN Preventative Deployment Force
UNPROFOR	UN Protection Force (Bosnia)
UNSCR	UN Security Council Resolution
WMD	Weapons of mass destruction

Chapter One

INTRODUCTION

In their classic work *Deterrence in American Foreign Policy*, Alexander George and Richard Smoke noted that deterrence, although inherently complex in application, was conceptually simple: "the persuasion of one's opponent that the costs and/or risks of a given course of action he might take outweigh its benefits."[1] George and Smoke explored the historical evolution of deterrence theory from its origins in theories about the balance of military power among states and coalitions to the advent of strategic bombing, whose coercive power was great even before nuclear weapons.[2] They argued that the nuclear revolution ushered in an era fundamentally different from those preceding it because of the new capability "to hurt an enemy grievously before (or without) destroying his military capability. . . . With the opening up of this possibility, the *threat* to hurt him could be separated—in fact and therefore in theory—from the threat to engage his forces." Thus, "Deterrence was conceived in its modern sense when it became possible to threaten vast damage and pain while leaving opposing military forces intact."[3]

Deterrence in American Foreign Policy was published in 1974, when the military context of the Cold War was dominated by two superpowers, the United States and the Soviet Union, within a deterrence regime largely bounded by nuclear weapons. Thus, a political-

---

[1]Alexander L. George and Richard Smoke, *Deterrence in American Foreign Policy: Theory and Practice* (New York: Columbia University Press, 1974), p. 11.

[2]Ibid., pp. 11–34.

[3]Ibid., p. 21. See also George Quester, *Deterrence Before Hiroshima* (New Brunswick, N.J.: Transaction Books, 1986).

military reality evolved in which "fear of escalation to global nuclear war was an inhibiting factor for both superpowers" and rules existed that "placed limits on what either superpower could safely do in situations where the other had clear stakes."[4]

Since the end of the Cold War, and the demise of the Soviet Union, the threat of large-scale nuclear war has largely receded and the United States has become the sole remaining superpower. Richard Haass argues that "liberated from the danger that military action will lead to confrontation with a rival superpower, the United States is now more free to intervene."[5] Indeed, the United States now possesses unprecedented *conventional* military capacity to carry out deterrent strategies because it has the capacity to launch crippling conventional attacks with virtual impunity on an adversary's homeland and his deployed military forces—or to threaten such attacks as a form of coercion.

The changes in the international security environment that characterize the post–Cold War era, however, have also added complexity to the strategic equations facing the United States. Haass identifies five characteristics of the current environment that increase the "potential for international challenges and crises":[6]

- Less political control and a diffusion of political authority as a result of the breakup of the Cold War blocs.

- Nationalism defined by ethnicity, rather than political ideology or territory, that raises the specter of cross-border aggression, internal conflicts, and refugee and humanitarian crises.

- The revival of traditional great power politics, wherein allies and former foes are willing to act in their own narrow self-interest rather than for or against U.S. positions.

---

[4]Richard N. Haass, *Intervention: The Use of American Military Force in the Post-Cold War World*, revised edition (Washington, D.C.: Brookings Institution Press, 1999), p. 3.

[5]Ibid., p. 8. This is not to suggest, however, that conventional deterrence is a post–Cold War development. Even at the height of the U.S.-Soviet rivalry, conventional military capabilities and threats often loomed large, notwithstanding the shadow of nuclear escalation.

[6]Ibid., p. 3.

- The relative weakening of the nation-state as a result of the increasing influence of nonstate actors (e.g., regional organizations, the United Nations, the International Monetary Fund, nongovernmental organizations, transnational corporations) challenging governmental authority.

- The international diffusion of military power as a result of the proliferation of advanced conventional and unconventional weapons of mass destruction (WMD).[7]

Thus, the United States, despite its unrivalled political and military power, faces an international security environment inherently more ambiguous and potentially less stable than at any time since the end of World War II. Furthermore, because of the inherent complexity of the situation—coupled with the absence of the organizing intellectual construct for the uses of national power that guided the containment of the Soviet Union during the Cold War—the United States has found itself largely in a reactive posture, forced to deal with each challenge on a case-by-case basis as it arises, and often on short notice.[8]

Many policy questions indicate that the security environment will become increasingly complex and that the challenges facing the United States will further multiply in the future.[9] Several of these come readily to mind. How will the United States deter, manage, and react to attacks on the U.S. homeland? What will be the U.S. response to the threat or use of chemical, biological, or nuclear weapons by an adversary? How can international alliances function in the absence of a common threat and with diffuse national interests among potential allies? What indeed are "vital interests" in the

---

[7]Ibid., pp. 3–5. In addition to the points Haass raises, there may also be instances where states or coalitions of states act in the absence of the United States in the pursuit of their individual or collective interests—e.g., the European Union.

[8]Ibid., p. 7.

[9]For examples, see Francis Fukuyama, *The End of History and the Last Man* (New York: Avon Books, 1992); Samuel P. Huntington, *The Clash of Civilizations and the Remaking of World Order* (New York: Simon & Schuster, 1996); Robert D. Kaplan, *The Coming Anarchy: Shattering the Dreams of the Post Cold War* (New York: Vintage Books, 2000); and the report by the U.S. Commission on National Security/21st Century, *Seeking a National Strategy: A Concert for Preserving Security and Promoting Freedom* (Washington, D.C., 2000).

absence of a threat to national survival or an ideological imperative? What is the "interest threshold" at which the United States will use military power as a coercive instrument? Policy options to address these questions, and others, must be crafted within the constraints of limited political will and resources.

Political will is a critical factor. Although the United States is much freer to decide when and where it will become involved in the absence of superpower confrontation, it faces several constraints. Some of these are self-imposed. Because of the apparent marginality of the national interests involved and the controversial nature of many post–Cold War uses of military power (and their potential to unravel, as they did in Somalia), it is more difficult to forge political consensus to support deployments that are often open-ended. An assertive Congress and ubiquitous media scrutiny complicate decisionmaking and "policymakers have less latitude to pursue policies that are controversial, uncertain in outcome, and potentially expensive, as military interventions tend to be."[10] Finally, although the American public is far more willing to suffer military casualties in pursuit of important causes that offer the prospect of success than is often suggested, military operations in defense of minor interests will lose public support if they become expensive to carry out.[11]

Resources are also a concern. The discussions of military readiness during the 2000 U.S. presidential campaign—readiness diluted in the views of many by frequent deployments to conflicts of limited interest to the United States—highlighted sensitivities in this area.[12] Perspectives differ about the appropriate use of U.S. military forces in the future. On one hand, some advocate military engagement and forward presence as shaping forces and hedges against future

---

[10]Haass, *Intervention*, p. 7.

[11]Eric V. Larson, *Casualties and Consensus* (Santa Monica, Calif.: RAND, MR-726-RC, 1996).

[12]See, for example, Michael R. Gordon, "Bush Would Stop U.S. Peacekeeping in Balkan Fights," *New York Times*, October 21, 2000, and "From Social Security to Environment, the Candidates' Positions," *New York Times*, November 5, 2000. Although much has changed in the U.S. security environment since late 2000, the issues and beliefs raised in these arguments continue to face defense policymakers.

conflict.[13] On the other hand, some believe that the armed forces of the United States should be focused on deterring and fighting wars and that long-term peacekeeping should be handled by other nations.[14] Both perspectives, however, acknowledge resource limits. As Richard Haass has noted, although the United States is the sole remaining superpower, "We can do anything, but not everything."[15]

METHODOLOGY

The purpose of this study is to provide an introduction to the coercive use of conventional military power for military and civilian professionals involved in the practical application of such power, focusing on the relationship between force structure and coercive effectiveness. Here we define conventional military coercion as the use or the threat of use of conventional military force to deter or compel an adversary into complying with U.S. demands or to punish an adversary for actions already taken. This report employed two approaches to assess which force capabilities and conditions are most likely to coerce a potential enemy or lead to his early defeat. First, we reviewed the literature on coercion to identify relevant theory, developed working definitions, and located conflict databases and assessed their utility. Although we provide definitions for coercion that apply to all the elements of national power (diplomatic, economic, informational, and military), we concentrate on the utility of military power as a coercive instrument in deterrence and compellence—and if coercion fails, unconditional conflict termination. Second, we selected and analyzed cases (both U.S. and

---

[13]See The White House, *A National Security Strategy for a New Century* (Washington, D.C., 1999).

[14]See "Transcript, Condoleezza Rice on Governor George W. Bush's Foreign Policy, October 12, 2000," available at http://www.cfr.org/p/pubs/Rice_10-12-00_Transcript.html, accessed March 15, 2000.

[15]Haass, *Intervention*, p. 8. See also Cindy Williams, ed., *Holding the Line: U.S. Defense Alternatives for the Early 21st Century* (Cambridge, Mass.: MIT Press, 2001); U.S. National Defense Panel, *Transforming Defense: National Security in the 21st Century* (Washington, D.C., 1997); and Ashton B. Carter and John P. White, eds., *Keeping the Edge: Managing Defense for the Future* (Cambridge, Mass.: Harvard University Press, 2000) for a few examples of the many perspectives emerging on how the United States should reshape its national security strategy and its military forces to meet the demands of the future international security environment.

foreign, including successes and failures) that would provide insights into the utility of military forces for conventional coercion in four categories across the spectrum of military operations: stability and support operations (SASO), smaller-scale contingencies (SSCs), major theater wars (MTWs), and strikes and raids. The case analyses focused on

- assessing what form(s) of coercion, if any, were involved;
- distilling insights about why the coercion was successful or unsuccessful;
- describing the military forces employed in each case and determining which of their capabilities were most effective; and
- deriving insights from the cases that should be relevant in the future.

The next chapter of this report examines the theory of coercion on several levels, ranging from basic definitions to more detailed exploration of factors that affect an enemy's motivation to fight. It emphasizes the importance of combining assessments of an adversary's military capabilities with an understanding of his will to prevail in a coercive confrontation instead of treating these as separate issues. Chapter Three discusses the case studies, describing how they were selected and what they reveal about the use of military force in coercion across the spectrum of operations. In keeping with the focus of this project, the case study analyses emphasize the impact of the types of military forces employed on the success or failure of coercion strategies. Chapter Four concludes the analysis by discussing the implications of these theoretical and historical conclusions for the use of U.S. conventional military forces in the future. Finally, the Appendix provides narrative descriptions of the cases examined in Chapter Three, including descriptions of the forces employed in them, to provide historical context for readers not familiar with some of the cases and to serve as a starting point for those who may wish to explore these cases in greater detail.

Chapter Two

THE THEORY OF COERCION

COERCION THEORY AND UNITED STATES FOREIGN POLICY

Much of U.S. foreign policy, and most of U.S. security policy, is built either directly or indirectly around coercion. *Coercion* is causing someone to choose one course of action over another by making the choice preferred by the coercer appear more attractive than the alternative, which the coercer wishes to avoid. In the international arena, coercion seeks to change the behavior of states (or occasionally significant nonstate actors),[1] for example by deterring aggression or by compelling an enemy to surrender, although it may involve far less serious stakes. Regardless of the nature of the enemy and the objective of the policy, however, coercion takes the form of an explicit or implicit message that the target actor should do A rather than B because the consequences of B will be less favorable to him than the consequences of A.

Each of the instruments of national power—military, economic, diplomatic, and other informational tools—can be, and often is, employed coercively. This report concentrates on the use of military

---

[1]Most of the following discussion will refer to coercive targets as "states," because it is states that are most often the targets of U.S. military coercion. However, it is important to note that virtually everything true about coercing states also applies to international coercion directed against significant nonstate actors, such as revolutionary or insurgency movements, substate groups involved in civil wars or wars of secession, or major terrorist organizations. At the lower end of the spectrum of conflict (for example in SASO) it is common for such nonstate actors to be the coercive targets, as reflected in the case studies included in this project.

force to achieve important security objectives, but readers should keep in mind that most of what is true about military coercion also applies to the coercive use of economic sanctions and other tools of international policy.[2] Within the military arena, however, a good definition of coercion from which to proceed is that of a recent RAND study: "Coercion is the use of threatened force, including the limited use of actual force to back up the threat, to induce an adversary to behave differently than it otherwise would."[3]

As shown in Figure 2.1, coercion can be distinguished from two other categories of statecraft: persuasion and pure force. *Persuasion* is more subtle than coercion. Instead of trying to convince the target that complying with the coercer's demands will serve the adversary's own interests better than defying them would, a persuasive policy seeks to change what the target values or believes more fundamentally. Many relatively low-profile military activities have persuasive effects on other states and thus shape the strategic environment, but their effects are usually gradual, and they normally play little role in strategies to deal with crises. However, military strategists should not neglect them, for they may have a great deal to do with whether future crises occur in the first place.[4]

Unconditional action—*pure force* or *physical defeat,* in the military realm—is more direct than coercion. Instead of making the target choose one course of action over another, it seeks to eliminate altogether the target's ability or opportunity to do anything other than

---

[2]Jonathan Kirshner, "The Microfoundations of Economic Sanctions," *Security Studies,* Vol. 6, No. 3 (Spring 1997), pp. 32–64.

[3]Daniel L. Byman, Matthew C. Waxman, and Eric Larson, *Air Power as a Coercive Instrument* (Santa Monica, Calif.: RAND, MR-1061-AF, 1999), p. 10.

[4]The distinction between coercion and persuasion can perhaps be illustrated more clearly in the context of the other major field of deterrence policy: deterring crime. Threats of punishment for criminals are obviously coercive and so are efforts to either convince potential wrongdoers that crime does not pay or bribe them to obey the law: Telling a teenager that he will end up wealthier by pursuing a lawful career than by turning to crime seeks to alter his expectations about which course will better serve his needs as he perceives them. Persuasion would involve making him place a lower value on whatever he might expect to gain from crime and causing him to place a higher value on the benefits to be expected from a noncriminal path. The third option, simply preventing him from having access to the tools or opportunities required for a criminal career, would fall into the realm of unconditional action.

RAND*MR1494-2.1*

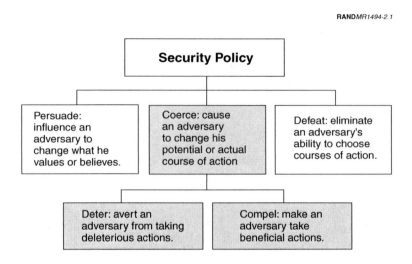

Figure 2.1—Components of Security Policy

what the attacker demands, or else it simply seizes or eliminates the subject of the dispute.[5] Armed forces have been employed to achieve major objectives through pure force in situations ranging from the U.S. invasion of Grenada in 1983 to Israel's 1981 attack on the Osirak nuclear reactor.[6] More often, however, substantial wars are won—or prevented—through coercion for the simple reason that it is usually less expensive to convince someone to surrender, or not to attack in the first place, than it is to make aggression or resistance physically impossible. Therefore, in most conflicts against capable adversaries, the primary strategic objective is to make the enemy accede to one's

---

[5]Thomas C. Schelling, *Arms and Influence* (New Haven, Conn.: Yale University Press, 1966). Of course, some direct military actions do not involve the application of force at all, such as delivering humanitarian assistance to victims of famine or natural disasters.

[6]The Osirak raid was intended to destroy the target and thus temporarily cripple Iraq's nuclear weapons program, and Israel presumably did not expect it to discourage Baghdad from continuing to pursue nuclear weapons development or to intimidate Iraq into a less anti-Israeli foreign policy (although Israeli leaders may have hoped that it would have a secondary coercive effect by discouraging other Middle Eastern states from building their own nuclear weapons facilities).

coercive demands, even if this is a demand for unconditional surrender.[7] However, if the stakes are very high for the enemy, for example when surrender is likely to mean certain death for the enemy leadership, it may be very difficult or even impossible to make the adversary give up short of utter defeat, and victory may only be achieved in the end through pure force.[8]

Deterrence

Within the realm of coercion, it is customary to distinguish between *deterrence* and *compellence*. According to one widely used definition, deterrence is "the persuasion of one's opponent that the costs and/or risks of a given course of action he might take outweigh its benefits."[9] However, because this definition does not explicitly consider the opponent's expectations about what will happen if it does not act, it may be clearer to describe deterrence as convincing someone not to take a contemplated action, such as attacking you, by making the expected results of the action appear worse than the expected consequences of not acting.

Perhaps no other concept in international politics has been the subject of as much academic and policy discussion as deterrence, so it is not surprising that other definitions of the term exist.[10] Some theo-

---

[7] Pure force objectives may exist within a coercive strategy, however, as exemplified by U.S. strategy in the 1991 Persian Gulf War. The primary goal was to coerce Iraq into withdrawing from Kuwait, but in the process the United States hoped to destroy Iraq's facilities for developing WMD and to wreck its conventional offensive military capabilities.

[8] "A vivid example of this distinction appears in the 1964 James Bond movie 'Goldfinger.' After being captured in the middle of the film, Bond is seen strapped to a table as a sinister-looking industrial laser cuts its way towards his center of gravity. Observing the beam's approach with considerable unease and misinterpreting it as a coercive threat, Bond asks the title villain 'Do you expect me to talk?' 'No, Mister Bond,' Goldfinger replies, 'I expect you to die'" (Karl Mueller, "Strategies of Coercion: Denial, Punishment, and the Future of Air Power," *Security Studies*, Vol. 7, No. 3 [Spring 1998], p. 184n).

[9] Alexander George and Richard Smoke, *Deterrence in American Foreign Policy*, p. 11.

[10] For overviews of the development of deterrence theory, which a study of this size cannot begin to provide, see Robert Jervis, "Deterrence Theory Revisited," *World Politics*, Vol. 31, No. 2 (January 1979), pp. 289–324; Fred Kaplan, *The Wizards of Armageddon* (New York: Simon & Schuster, 1983); Lawrence Freedman, *The Evolution of Nuclear Strategy*, second edition (New York: St. Martin's Press, 1989); and John Har-

rists have argued that deterrence must involve threats of military force in particular,[11] or even more particularly only threats of nuclear attack,[12] or only threats of punishment directly against civilian populations and governments.[13] However, the most useful definitions of deterrence are broad ones, which acknowledge that such actions as aggression may be deterred by many means; never has this been truer than in the post–Cold War era.[14] These means may even include promises of rewards for complying with coercive demands because making compliance with one's demands more attractive has essentially the same effect as making defiance less attractive.[15]

Although deterrence is most often discussed in the context of deterring potential aggressors from launching invasions or committing other breaches of the peace, deterrence is not something that occurs only at the boundary between peace and war. Security policymakers may also work to deter target states—both enemies and friends—from such peacetime actions as acquiring WMD or entering into threatening alliances. In wartime, deterrent efforts often occur within the conflict, as belligerents and nonbelligerents seek to deter other states from such actions as escalating to higher levels of violence, expanding the war into new arenas, or violating the laws of armed conflict or neutrality.

---

vey, *Conventional Deterrence and National Security* (Canberra, Australia: RAAF Air Power Studies Centre, 1997).

[11]Patrick Morgan, *Deterrence: A Conceptual Analysis* (Beverly Hills, Calif.: Sage Publications, 1983), pp. 20–22; Paul K. Huth, *Extended Deterrence and the Prevention of War* (New Haven, Conn.: Yale University Press, 1988), p. 15.

[12]Until the late 1970s, most deterrence scholarship focused primarily—and often exclusively—on issues of nuclear strategy. Prominent steps toward serious consideration of purely conventional deterrence include George Quester, *Deterrence Before Hiroshima,* and John J. Mearsheimer, *Conventional Deterrence* (Ithaca, N.Y.: Cornell University Press, 1983). For an overview of conventional deterrence theory, see Harvey, *Conventional Deterrence and National Security.*

[13]Stephen J. Cimbala, *Strategy After Deterrence* (New York: Praeger, 1991), pp. xi–xii.

[14]For example, Thomas W. Milburn, "What Constitutes Effective Deterrence?" *Journal of Conflict Resolution*, Vol. 3, No. 2 (June 1959), pp. 138–145; Samuel P. Huntington, "The Renewal of Strategy," in Samuel P. Huntington, ed., *The Strategic Imperative* (Cambridge, Mass.: Ballinger, 1982), pp. 14–17; and Mearsheimer, *Conventional Deterrence*, pp. 14–15.

[15]Paul Huth and Bruce Russett, "Testing Deterrence Theory: Rigor Makes a Difference," *World Politics*, Vol. 42, No. 4 (July 1990), pp. 469–471.

Deterrence, like all coercion, occurs in the mind of the adversary. Reality matters in deterrence only insofar as it affects the perceptions of those who will choose whether or not to be deterred. Thus, a fundamental difference exists between the concepts of deterrence and defense: deterrence seeks to make conflict look bad to the enemy, while defense seeks to make conflict better for oneself if conflict occurs. Bluffs may deter, but they will not contribute to defense if deterrence fails, while military capabilities kept secret from the enemy may provide defense, but cannot deter.[16] The psychological nature of coercion greatly complicates the problem of anticipating when coercive strategies will succeed or fail. Traditional assessments of the adversary's capabilities are of only limited predictive value unless accompanied by sound understanding of what the enemy values, how it perceives the conflict, and how it makes decisions—to name but a few of the critical variables.

Because of its focus on U.S. security concerns, this study emphasizes *extended deterrence*—that is, deterring attacks against allies and other external interests rather than direct attacks against the deterring state. In general, extended deterrence is more difficult than simple self-protective deterrence because a potential aggressor is more likely to doubt that costly threats will actually be carried out in response to an attack against a far-flung or less-than-vital interest.

It can also be useful to distinguish between *strategic* and *tactical deterrence*. Most deterrence of concern to military strategists is strategic-level: efforts to cause changes in the behavior of states or other major entities that operate in the international arena.[17] However, tactical deterrence, which involves the immediate behavior of individual people or small groups—the sort of deterrence that most police officers (and parents) routinely deal with—sometimes can have outcomes with important strategic implications, especially in

---

[16]Glenn H. Snyder, *Deterrence and Defense* (Princeton, N.J.: Princeton University Press, 1961), Chapter 1.

[17]This does not necessarily require that the adversary be a unitary actor. Deterring an adversary might involve changing the policy preferences of several different, perhaps even competing, substate actors or interest groups within it, which may respond in different ways to particular deterrence measures. On the need to disaggregate the enemy, and the challenges of doing so, see Kirshner, "Microfoundations of Economic Sanctions."

peacekeeping and related operations. Although strategic and tactical deterrence have many similarities, the two can differ significantly because of the nature of the actors involved and the kinds of pressures that can be applied to them. In particular, psychological factors are likely to loom larger and work differently in shaping the results of tactical coercion against individuals than they do in coercion of states or large groups that are governed by more complex decisionmaking bodies.[18] In some conflicts, both types of deterrence will be important. In others, central authorities may have virtually complete control over the tactical actions of their subordinates, so only strategic deterrence will really matter. But when the policy objective depends on shaping the behavior of individuals or small groups operating independently of higher authority, the tactical level of deterrence may be the only one in play.

Compellence

Whereas deterrence seeks to dissuade the target from doing something the coercer wishes to avoid, compellence attempts to make the target change its behavior in accordance with the coercer's demands—for example, to halt an invasion, to withdraw from disputed territory, or to surrender.[19] However, almost everything true about deterrence applies to compellence as well, though not always in exactly the same way. Moreover, the line separating the two categories is not always clear. For example, as Thomas Schelling observes, a demand that an invader not proceed beyond a particular geographic threshold can be interpreted with equal plausibility

---

[18]This is not a true dichotomy, of course. When national decisions are made by a single individual, strategic deterrence is likely to resemble tactical deterrence more than when national decisions are in the hands of a large, bureaucratized government, for example. On the role of psychological factors in coercion, see, for example, Robert Jervis, *Perception and Misperception in International Politics* (Princeton, N.J.: Princeton University Press, 1976); Robert Jervis, Richard Ned Lebow, and Janice Gross Stein, eds., *Psychology and Deterrence* (Baltimore: Johns Hopkins University Press, 1985); and Irving L. Janis and Leon Mann, *Decision Making* (New York: The Free Press, 1977).

[19]Some theorists (for example, Robert A. Pape, *Bombing to Win: Air Power and Coercion in War* [Ithaca, N.Y.: Cornell University Press, 1996]) refer to compellence (a term coined by Thomas Schelling) simply as coercion, on the grounds that this is consistent with the colloquial meaning of coercion. However, doing so leaves no term to attach to the combined category of coercion (i.e., deterrence and compellence) as described here, which is the reason Schelling introduced the new word in the first place.

either as compelling the enemy to halt his advance or as deterring him from advancing further.[20]

In compellence, as in deterrence, successful threats do not have to be carried out. However, violence may be used to make the threat, particularly in compellence. While deterrent threats take the form "if you do A, I will do B," compellent threats are often open-ended: "until you do X, I will do Y."[21] This approach to compellence is risky because it cedes the initiative to the adversary, who can choose how long to resist the coercer's demands and thus how high the cost of the compellent policy will be. Because of this, it may be more attractive to threaten discrete compellent actions, along the lines of "unless you do X by my deadline, I will do Y."

Other things being equal, compellence tends to be more difficult than deterrence. It is usually easier to make a potential aggressor decide not to attack in the first place than it is to cause the same aggressor to call off the attack once it is under way, for a variety of fairly obvious reasons, such as the political and psychic costs of reversing a policy after it is publicly embarked upon. If the coercer is demanding that the adversary abandon a war or some other effort that has already cost a great deal of blood or treasure and the pursuit of which has involved intense mobilization of nationalist or religious sentiment, success may be especially hard to achieve. Once a conflict is over, observers almost always conclude that the war should have ended sooner than it did, if only the losing side had been less reluctant to admit that the situation had become hopeless.[22]

The characteristic perhaps most often associated with compellence in the popular imagination is the gradual escalation of force, as discussed prominently in the work of Thomas Schelling. This approach was famously used during Operation Rolling Thunder, the U.S.

---

[20]Schelling, *Arms and Influence*, p. 77; Byman, Waxman, and Larson, *Air Power as a Coercive Instrument*, pp. 11–12.

[21]An equally important but often ignored element of the coercive threat is its second half: "and if you comply with my demands, I will not do B (or will stop doing Y)." If the target does not expect that punishment is conditional upon its behavior, there is no incentive to comply. Thus, any coercive threat also involves a corresponding promise, and the credibility of each matters (as will be discussed below).

[22]Pape, *Bombing to Win*, pp. 32–35.

bombing of North Vietnam in 1965–1968, and its spectacular lack of success in that costly campaign permanently discredited gradual escalation, and with it the compellent use of force more generally, in the eyes of many American military strategists.[23] However, this is an intellectual mistake on two levels. First, the failure of Operation Rolling Thunder stemmed from many factors, and while some of them related to the particular ways in which gradualism was applied against Hanoi, the outcome of this single campaign by no means demonstrated that gradual escalation is always doomed to fail.[24] Second, and more important in the context of this report, compellence need not involve gradual escalation. Indeed, coercive force can be applied in virtually unlimited ways, although when states perceive that they can achieve their objectives through limited (and thus typically less costly) use of force, they are likely to take advantage of the opportunity.

COERCIVE STRATEGY

Coercion depends on making the target decide that acquiescence is a better course of action than defying the coercer's demands. In deterrence, this means making the expected value of aggression (or whatever else is being deterred) appear worse than the expected value of the status quo. In compellence, it means making the value of resistance appear worse than the value of compliance. How attractive aggression or resistance appears will depend in turn on three factors: the expected benefits if the action is ultimately successful, the expected costs of the policy, and the expected probability of succeeding at it.[25]

---

[23]On Rolling Thunder, see Mark Clodfelter, *The Limits of Air Power: The American Bombing of North Vietnam* (New York: The Free Press, 1989), and Wallace J. Thies, *When Governments Collide: Coercion and Diplomacy in the Vietnam Conflict, 1964–1968* (Berkeley, Calif.: University of California Press, 1980).

[24]Peter W. Huggins, *Airpower and Gradual Escalation: Reconsidering the Conventional Wisdom* (master's thesis, School of Advanced Airpower Studies, 2000).

[25]This can be represented symbolically, for those who are so inclined, in the following inequality:

$$B_C - C_C > P_S(B_{SR} - C_{SR}) + (1 - P_S)(B_{UR} - C_{UR}),$$

where B is expected benefits, C is expected costs, C_C indicates the results of complying with the coercive demands, $_{SR}$ and $_{UR}$ indicate the results of successful and unsuccessful resistance, and P_S is the estimated probability that resistance will succeed.

There are thus three principal approaches to coercion. *Accommodation*, also known as "positive deterrence," offers incentives for complying with the coercive demands.[26] Although this approach is often the most effective and efficient way to achieve coercive objectives, either alone or in a "carrot and stick" combination with other coercive measures, it does not typically involve a large role for military forces, so it will not be a major focus of this study.

Punishment is the strategy most strongly associated with coercion: threatening to impose high costs on the adversary if it does not comply with the coercive demands. Punishment may involve threatening to kill or harm civilian populations, to kill soldiers in combat, or virtually any other threat to inflict harm against something that the enemy decisionmakers value. In its purest form, punitive coercion does not limit the enemy's ability to act but instead seeks to destroy the will to do so by making the effort appear too expensive to be worthwhile.[27]

Coercion by *denial,* in contrast, seeks to convince the adversary that resisting the coercer's demands will be unsuccessful. This typically involves threatening to defeat an enemy on the battlefield, although denial may take other forms instead, depending on the enemy's

---

Coercion should be successful if the left side of the inequality is greater than the right. For the specific case of deterring aggression, substitute SQ (status quo) for C, V (victory) for S and SR, and D (defeat) for UR. Extreme risk acceptance or aversion can be represented by increasing or discounting the values attached to the appropriate costs and benefits. (See Karl Mueller, "Strategy, Asymmetric Deterrence, and Accommodation," Ph.D. dissertation, Princeton University, 1991.)

In using such formulas, however, Glenn Snyder's timeless caveat should be borne firmly in mind: "The numerical illustrations are intended simply to set out as starkly as possible the essential logic of deterrence; there is no intent to light a torch for the 'quantifiability' of the factors involved, which are of course, highly intangible, unpredictable, unmeasurable, and incommensurable except in an intuitive way" (Snyder, *Deterrence and Defense*, p. 16n).

[26]Milburn, "What Constitutes Effective Deterrence?" As noted above, many deterrence theorists reject including reassurance or promises of reward under the heading of coercion. This prejudice is less common among scholars of international political economy. See also David A. Baldwin, "The Power of Positive Sanctions," *World Politics*, Vol. 24, No. 1 (October 1971), pp. 19–38, and Mueller, "Strategy, Asymmetric Deterrence, and Accommodation."

[27]Schelling, *Arms and Influence*; Quester, *Deterrence Before Hiroshima*; and Mearsheimer, *Conventional Deterrence*.

strategy.[28] Where punishment seeks to coerce the enemy through fear, denial depends on causing hopelessness. Of course, punishment and denial strategies often overlap because defeating an enemy almost always inflicts damage along the way, while many forms of punishment will also make some contribution to convincing the enemy that defeat is inevitable.[29]

Because coercion depends on the adversary weighing the expected results of several courses of action and then choosing the more attractive one, it presumes that policy decisions are made with some degree of rationality.[30] However, the adversary need not behave with perfect rationality for coercion to be applicable, its behavior simply must not be totally irrational. The more rational the adversary, the more predictable its behavior may be, but departures from ideal rationality may make it either easier or more difficult to coerce. In practice, no state acts perfectly rational, stemming from such factors as incomplete information, limited time to make decisions, bureaucratic politics and organizational processes, and leaders' personalities. Yet states (and significant nonstate political entities) rarely act in ways that appear truly unreasoning on close analysis.[31]

It is far more common for states' actions to be branded as irrational when they are actually being driven by logical and consistent sets of preferences, but these are not well understood by others.[32] It is not

---

[28]Snyder, *Deterrence and Defense;* Adam Roberts, *Nations in Arms,* second edition (London: Macmillan, 1986); Pape, *Bombing to Win.*

[29]There is a fourth possible approach to coercion: convincing the enemy that even if it succeeds, the benefits will be small, for example by threatening to destroy assets that an invader covets. Although there have been interesting cases of such coercion strategies, they typically depend upon the existence of relatively unusual circumstances. For further discussion of these approaches, see Mueller, "Strategies of Coercion."

[30]See George Downs, "The Rational Deterrence Debate," *World Politics,* Vol. 41, No. 2 (January 1989), pp. 225–237.

[31]On the problems of assessing an adversary's interests and inclinations in the face of real-world obstacles, and some approaches to overcoming them, see Paul K. Davis, "Improving Deterrence in the Post-Cold War Era," in Paul K. Davis, ed., *New Challenges for Defense Planning: Rethinking How Much Is Enough* (Santa Monica, Calif.: RAND, MR-400-RC, 1994), pp. 197–222.

[32]Kenneth Watman, Dean Wilkening, John Arquilla, and Brian Nichiporuk, *U.S. Regional Deterrence Strategies* (Santa Monica, Calif.: RAND, MR-490-A/AF, 1995); Yehezkel Dror, *Crazy States: A Counterconventional Strategic Problem* (Milwood, N.Y.: Kraus, 1980).

irrational to either prefer death before dishonor or to prefer the opposite. Because coercion depends entirely on the target state's choices, a poor grasp of what the adversary values and how it makes decisions can easily be a recipe for strategic failure, as well as bewilderment. Such misperceptions may not only cause coercion to fail where it is expected to succeed but may also lead to policies that have effects opposite to those intended.[33]

Coercion Outcomes

Assessing whether a coercion policy was successful can be a difficult task. Compellence results are often ambiguous, especially when some of the coercer's demands are met but others are not. Even when coercion succeeds, deciding how much to credit the coercion policy can be a problem because it is often difficult to be sure that the same outcome would not have resulted from a different policy or even no policy effort at all. This issue arises particularly in cases of successful deterrence, such as the U.S. effort to deter an Iraqi invasion of Saudi Arabia in 1990, where it may not be clear whether the potential aggressor was seriously considering attacking in the first place. Even when a coercion strategy can clearly be credited with success, which of its elements were necessary to produce the outcome and which were superfluous may remain the subject of active debate for years or decades afterward, even when the leaders who made the key decisions provide firsthand testimony.[34]

When assessing the merits of coercion strategies, it is also important not entirely to conflate the success or failure of coercion with the

---

[33]Of course, inadequate understanding of one's own strengths, weaknesses, and values can also be a recipe for failure.

[34]For example, Pape, *Bombing to Win*; Barry D. Watts, "Ignoring Reality: Problems of Theory and Evidence in Security Studies," *Security Studies*, Vol. 7, No. 2 (Winter 1997/98), pp. 115–171; Robert A. Pape, "The Air Force Strikes Back: A Reply to Barry Watts and John Warden," *Security Studies*, Vol. 7, No. 2 (Winter 1997/98), pp. 191–214; Mueller, "Strategies of Coercion"; Barton J. Bernstein, "Compelling Japan's Surrender Without the A-Bomb, Soviet Entry, or Invasion: Reconsidering the US Bombing Survey's Early-Surrender Conclusions," *Journal of Strategic Studies*, Vol. 18, No. 2 (June 1995), pp. 101–148; Daniel L. Byman and Matthew C. Waxman, "Kosovo and the Great Air Power Debate," *International Security*, Vol. 24, No. 4 (Spring 2000), pp. 5–38; and Stephen T. Hosmer, *The Conflict over Kosovo: Why Milosevic Decided to Settle When He Did* (Santa Monica, Calif.: RAND, MR-1351-AF, 2001).

success or failure of the overall strategy. For example, a strategy may fail to coerce the adversary, yet make a significant contribution to a larger effort that achieved its objectives, as in the case of the Allied air campaign against Germany in World War II.[35] Or a strategy may fail to coerce its apparent target (or never have been truly intended to do so), yet have important coercive effects on other audiences.[36] On the other hand, a strategy may achieve its coercive objectives yet be accounted a failure in the long term because of its indirect results or the fleeting nature of its success.[37]

Although many studies have sought to identify factors that can explain and predict the success or failure of coercion strategies, none has identified a simple and reliable recipe for success.[38] However, a number of patterns have emerged. As a first approximation, it can be said that the effectiveness of a coercive threat is a function of the target's perception of the coercer's capability, the credibility of the threat, its severity relative to the stakes in the confrontation, and the target's ability to respond to the strategy with coercion of its own.

Capability

Capability was not the central concern of U.S. deterrence theorists during the height of the Cold War, because the ability of the super-powers to carry out their nuclear threats was often, though not always, taken for granted. The less a coercion situation resembles the U.S.-Soviet nuclear standoff, however, the more important assessments of capability become, for two reasons. One is that the milder a threat is, the more willing the target state may be to take a

---

[35]Richard J. Overy, *Why the Allies Won* (New York: W. W. Norton and Company, 1995).

[36]Thomas P. Ehrhard, *Making the Connection: An Air Strategy Analysis Framework* (Maxwell AFB, Ala.: Air University Press, 1995).

[37]Examples in this category range from the Soviet defeat of Finland in 1940 to the 1991 UN intervention in Somalia, which initially was a spectacular success, saving many lives at very low cost.

[38]For example: George and Smoke, *Deterrence in American Foreign Policy;* Alexander L. George and William E. Simons, eds., *The Limits of Coercive Diplomacy*, second edition (Boulder, Colo.: Westview, 1994); Mearsheimer, *Conventional Deterrence;* Huth, *Extended Deterrence and the Prevention of War;* Pape, *Bombing to Win;* Peter Viggo Jakobsen, *Western Use of Coercive Diplomacy After the Cold War* (New York: St. Martin's Press, 1998).

chance that it cannot actually be carried out, a subject to which we will return shortly. The other is that conventional military threats are, on the whole, more vulnerable to being foiled by defensive measures than are threats of nuclear attack, which encourages targets not only to question coercers' ability to carry out their threats, but also to develop countermeasures instead of accepting their own vulnerability.[39]

It is also important to note that what matters is not raw military capability in the purest sense, but instead the capability that the coercer can realistically bring to bear in a particular situation. A variety of domestic and external factors may effectively limit one's capabilities and, although these constraints are likely to be less severe the higher the stakes are for the coercer, rarely are they entirely absent. For example, in many crises it is inconceivable that the United States would employ nuclear weapons, so the U.S. nuclear arsenal becomes irrelevant to assessments of U.S. capabilities in those cases.

Credibility

The credibility of coercive threats is central to deterrence theory because the efficacy of a threat depends not only on whether the coercer appears capable of carrying it out but also on whether it appears likely to do so. (As discussed earlier, whether the coercer actually will carry out its threat is irrelevant, the question is what the target believes that it will do.) Coercive threats need not be entirely believable, however. Even a very small chance that a coercer will follow through on a threat to inflict great harm, such as launching a nuclear attack, may carry considerable coercive weight. Generally, the more frightening a threatened action is, the less credible it needs to be. Conversely, more severe threats are typically (but not always) more expensive to carry out. When this is so, they are less likely to be entirely credible than milder ones because the coercer has greater incentives to renege on costly threats than inexpensive ones.[40]

---

[39]Richard J. Harknett, "The Logic of Conventional Deterrence," *Security Studies*, Vol. 4, No. 1 (Autumn 1994), pp. 86–114, refers to this property as "contestability."

[40]Not all threats are expensive to execute, however. See, for example, Jonathan Kirshner, *Currency and Coercion* (Princeton, N.J.: Princeton University Press, 1995), Chap-

With many deterrent threats, credibility depends not only on the apparent will to act, but also on an apparent will to act with persistence. If the target believes that the coercer will deploy troops, establish a blockade, or impose economic sanctions but expects that the coercer will soon tire of the policy and abandon it, the credibility of the initial threat is likely to count for little.[41]

Coercers seek to increase the credibility of their threats by a wide variety of means.[42] Many of these involve making it harder not to carry out their threats by creating situations in which it would be politically costly or physically impossible to back down. For example, to bolster extended deterrence, states may deploy "trip wire" forces in the line of a potential aggressor's advance against an ally, signaling that once lives had been lost, the deterrer could not fail to continue fighting against the enemy that had attacked its own troops.[43] In some cases, giving the enemy information about one's plans or capabilities may enhance credibility because what is not known cannot coerce. In others cases, coercive credibility may benefit from ambiguity. For example, if accurate information would reveal the actual weakness of one's strength or resolve, capabilities or intentions left unclear may be more frightening.

What Is at Stake for the Enemy?

There is more to coercion than making credible threats and having the apparent ability to carry them out, however. It is also necessary to threaten the target with something worse than the results of complying with the coercive demands. This requires the coercer to understand what the enemy values: not only how much it values what is being threatened, but also how committed it will be to resisting the coercion. Some demands may be so severe than no possible

---

ter Three. Conversely, making a threat less costly to carry out will not necessarily make it more credible—the target may interpret very inexpensive threats as a signal that the coercer lacks the will to act at all.

[41]William E. Herr, *Operation Vigilant Warrior: Conventional Deterrence Theory, Doctrine, and Practice* (Maxwell AFB, Ala.: Air University Press, 1997).

[42]See especially Schelling, *Arms and Influence.*

[43]Of course, if the foe believes that inflicting casualties against the deterrer will instead break its will to fight, such a strategy would be far less appealing.

coercive pressure will be sufficient to produce compliance.[44] Indeed, in many cases of unsuccessful coercion, the coercer's threats were entirely credible and were even carried out exactly as promised but simply were not substantial enough to tip the target's calculus in favor of surrender.[45] When the stakes are very high, punishment strategies will rarely succeed, at least on their own, because even a very small chance of eventually prevailing may well be enough to motivate the target to resist, even if this requires paying a high price.[46]

Success may also depend on creating a sense of urgency in the adversary, a belief that not only is complying with the coercer's demands sensible but that doing so quickly will be better than delaying the capitulation.[47] This may be accomplished by presenting a deadline or ultimatum, after which the conflict will escalate or the demands will increase, or by inflicting high ongoing costs that the target will be anxious to bring to an end. However, in some cases a deadline might instead provoke an opponent into a preemptive attack or other actions intended to head off the approaching disaster before the window of opportunity closes.[48]

Coercion and Countercoercion

Finally, coercers should recognize that coercion, particularly compellence, is a two-way street. While the coercer seeks to compel the

---

[44]Michael Brown, *Deterrence Failures and Deterrence Strategies* (Santa Monica, Calif.: RAND, P-5842, 1977).

[45]Classic examples include Israel's failure to deter Egyptian attack in 1973, the U.S. grain embargo and Olympic boycott against the Soviet Union following the 1979 invasion of Afghanistan (although Washington can hardly have expected compellence to succeed in that case), and the UN sanctions to coerce Iraq into giving up its chemical and biological weapons in the wake of the 1991 Gulf War.

[46]Pape, *Bombing to Win*; Mueller, "Strategies of Coercion."

[47]George and Simons, *The Limits of Coercive Diplomacy.*

[48]Richard Ned Lebow, "Windows of Opportunity: Do States Jump Through Them?" *International Security*, Vol. 9, No. 1 (Summer 1984), pp. 147–186, but see also Dan Reiter, "Exploding the Powder Keg Myth: Preemptive Wars Almost Never Happen," *International Security*, Vol. 20, No. 2 (Fall 1995), pp. 5–34. Japan's decision to attack the United States in 1941 is the archetypal example of such a case; see Scott Sagan, "From Deterrence to Coercion to War: The Road to Pearl Harbor," in George and Simons, *The Limits of Coercive Diplomacy.*

adversary to comply with its demands, the target will usually attempt to make the coercer abandon its effort or perhaps comply with its own set of more extensive demands.[49] Whichever party gives up first loses.[50]

A wide range of countercoercion strategies is possible. The target may seek to punish the coercer by striking at its military forces, its homeland, or anything else it values, using military, economic, or other means. It may concentrate its energies simply on resisting the coercive pressure applied against it, developing defenses and countermeasures and hoping to hold out longer than the coercer is able or willing to persist. Or it may seek to change the situation at the outset—for example, by striking quickly and presenting the coercer with a fait accompli before it can carry out its own preparations for the campaign.

Capability, vulnerability, will, and external constraints all matter in deciding the outcome of the contest. A state that cares far more about the issue in dispute than its adversary has a considerable advantage, but so does a state that can bring greater capabilities to bear or that faces fewer limitations in its employment of them. Any edge can help. In the end, coercion is most likely to succeed when the coercer can convince the target that resistance will be costly, success will be impossible, and the cost of complying with the coercive demands is a price that it can afford to pay. Coercion may succeed without achieving all of these conditions, particularly if the stakes are low, but failure to fulfill any of them may be sufficient to make a coercive strategy fail.

WHAT DOES IT TAKE TO COERCE?

To determine how and with what means to coerce an adversary, one must make two fundamental assessments. One is partly quantitative: an assessment of the capabilities possessed by the adversary

---

[49]Daniel L. Byman and Matthew C. Waxman, "Defeating U.S. Coercion," *Survival*, Vol. 41, No. 2 (Summer 1999), pp. 107–120.

[50]Of course, in practice such victories may be Pyrrhic and defeats may turn out to be for the best in the long run. Coercion is a competitive game but not always a simple one.

relative to those of the coercer. The other assessment is qualitative: an analysis of the adversary's deterrence/compellence threshold vis-à-vis the issue at stake (the context).[51] From this appreciation, a net assessment can be conducted to determine the adversary's strengths and weaknesses and what means will likely be necessary to coerce or defeat him.[52] In short, one must understand the adversary's will and his capabilities to be able to determine the resources and capabilities necessary to coerce him and, if coercion fails, to force him to meet your demands.

---

[51] Joint Chiefs of Staff, *Joint Publication 2-0: Doctrine for Intelligence Support* (Washington, D.C., 2000) and Joint Chiefs of Staff, *Joint Publication 2-02: National Intelligence Support to Joint Operations* (Washington, D.C., 1998) contain detailed descriptions of the U.S. intelligence agencies and of the processes and joint doctrine for intelligence support to interagency, joint, and multinational operation. See also Ashley J. Tellis et al., *Measuring National Power in the Postindustrial Age* (Santa Monica, Calif.: RAND, MR-1110-A, 2000). This study proposes a different analytic framework to understand "true" national power, noting the failure of existing frameworks to accurately measure the relative power of nations. As evidence, the authors note that the "Soviet Union and Iraq, classified as relatively significant powers by some aggregate indications of capability, either collapsed through internal enervation or proved utterly ineffectual when their capabilities were put to the test in war" (p. iii).

[52] See Department of Defense, Office of Net Assessment, "Fact Sheet: What Is Net Assessment?" (undated). This document offers the following definition of net assessment: "Broadly defined, a net assessment is an evaluation of the strengths and weakness of two or more competitors. In particular, net assessments involve a long-term and comprehensive *diagnosis* of that competition. These assessments are designed to highlight existing or emerging problem areas, or important opportunities that deserve top-level attention to improve the future US military position. Net assessments are inherently eclectic. In addition to models and simulations used in traditional systems analyses, a net assessment may be informed by contributions for the fields of demographics, economics, science and technology, sociology, political science, business, history and anthropology. Thus, the general characteristics of a net assessment are that of a long-term, holistic, multi-disciplinary study of national-level competition, rather than a simple 'snapshot' of the current situation and a prescriptive solution to the challenge at hand. Net assessments are designed primarily to inform senior decisionmakers responsible for long-range national security planning. The net assessment frames the state of the competition by identifying key long-term trends, major asymmetries in the capabilities of nations, as well as the operational concepts and strategies of the US and its adversaries that are relevant to the continuing competition. In the end, the decisionmakers are presented with the *net balance* of the strengths and weakness that emerges from this broad-based comparison, as well as a set of issues that are important for top-level officials to address concerning emerging threat areas or important opportunities. . . . The office [OSD Office of Net Assessment] provides the Secretary of Defense, military commanders, and other Department of Defense officials with assessments of military balance by major geographic theater or functional mission area." (Emphasis in the original.)

RAND senior scientist Paul Davis has analyzed the factors that contribute to an adversary's propensity for risk-taking behavior as a crucial factor in assessing his potential for aggression (Figure 2.2). [53]

Davis identifies several factors that shape the cost-benefit analysis used by a protagonist contemplating aggression, which represent important, specific manifestations of the general principles presented earlier in this chapter:

- **An assessment of the current situation and trends in the future.** If the assessment results in the conclusion that the status quo is unacceptable (or likely to become so) and that military action offers greater payoffs with acceptable risks, then aggression is more likely.

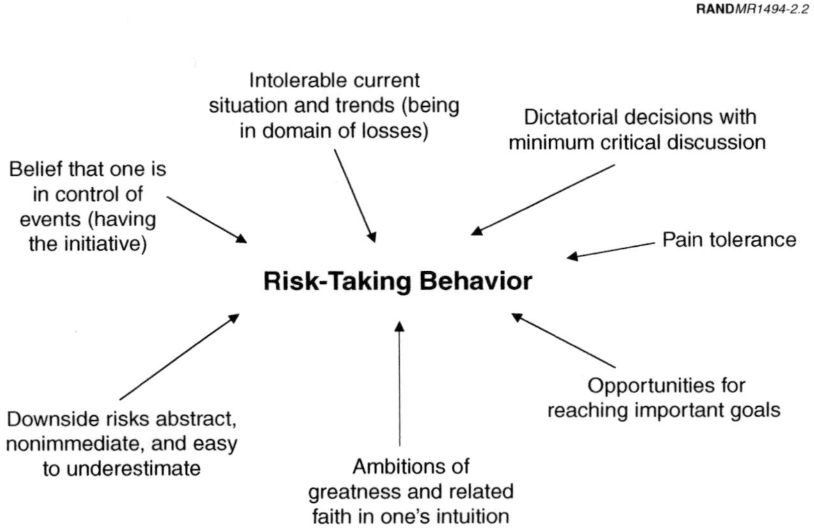

RAND*MR1494-2.2*

Intolerable current
situation and trends (being
in domain of losses)

Dictatorial decisions with
minimum critical discussion

Belief that one is
in control of
events (having
the initiative)

Pain tolerance

Risk-Taking Behavior

Downside risks abstract,
nonimmediate, and easy
to underestimate

Opportunities for
reaching important goals

Ambitions of
greatness and related
faith in one's intuition

Figure 2.2—Factors Contributing to Risk-Taking Behavior by an Adversary

---

[53]Davis, *New Challenges for Defense Planning*, pp. 209–210.

- **The degree to which decisions can be taken unilaterally (limiting discussion that might change perceptions).** The classic example here is that of Adolf Hitler, who made unilateral decisions about strategy (the invasion of the Soviet Union in particular) and did not allow discussion of potential risks, despite the existence of a professional German general staff, which rapidly came to understand Hitler's authority and assumed a largely sycophantic role.

- **Ability to tolerate pain.** The higher an adversary's tolerance for pain, the greater is his propensity to take risks. For example, the ability of the North Vietnamese to absorb years of bombing and attrition of their ground forces during the Vietnam War greatly exceeded the estimates of U.S. planners.[54]

- **The potential to achieve important goals.** The greater the prize, the more likely an aggressor will be to risk action. Paul Huth has noted the heightened propensity for aggression if "the decision to dispute territory could be linked to the expected political benefits of increased popular support and legitimacy when claims were directed at achieving national unification, the recovery of lost national territory, or gaining access to valuable economic resources."[55]

- **Ambition.** The more ambitious the adversary, the more likely he is to commit aggression. Davis cites the example of Saddam Hussein: "This is often underestimated in thinking about adver-

---

[54]See John E. Mueller, "The Search for the 'Breaking Point' in Vietnam: The Statistics of a Deadly Quarrel," *International Studies Quarterly,* Vol. 24 (December 1980), p. 499. Mueller notes that "American strategies for success in Vietnam were based on the central assumption that if the Communists sustained enough military punishment they would finally relent, forsaking (at least temporarily) their war effort." In short, the North Vietnamese had a "breaking point." Unfortunately for U.S. strategy, the North Vietnamese were committed to a protracted war, no matter how much pain was inflicted upon them. A statement by Vo Nguyen Giap, a principal North Vietnamese leader, showed the level of this commitment and his nation's ability to absorb pain: "Every minute, hundreds of thousands of people die all over the world. The life or death of a hundred, a thousand, or tens of thousands of human beings, even if they are our own compatriots, represents really very little" (quote from commentary by Robert Kromer in *The Lessons of Vietnam,* W. Scott Thompson and Donaldson D. Frizzell, eds. [New York: Crane, Russak, 1977], p. 77).

[55]Paul K. Huth, *Standing Your Ground: Territorial Disputes and International Conflict* (Ann Arbor, Mich.: University of Michigan Press, 1996), pp. 182–183.

saries in crisis and conflict. Status-quo powers fairly comfortable with their own circumstances are especially likely to underestimate others' ambitions. So it is that Saddam Hussein was erroneously assumed to be 'pragmatic' and to be merely looking for a way to improve Iraq's economic situation 'somewhat,' when in fact he had grandiose goals."[56]

- **The abstractness of risk factors.** The more remote or abstract the risk, the more it may be underestimated by someone who is yearning for action. This encourages quick and decisive action by aggressors because the perceived risks of immediate action are mitigated by the potential for gain, while longer-term abstract risks can be obscured by the present. For example, Saddam Hussein invaded Kuwait based on an assessment of the immediate risks of that action—without giving full consideration to the more remote and thus abstract risk of an eventual war with the United States.[57]

- **The belief that one is in control of events and has the initiative.** An adversary who believes he can "make his own luck" is more likely to commit aggression. The most obvious example is Adolf Hitler, who came to believe intensely in his own ability to overcome almost any obstacles in the path of his designs for German victory.[58]

Davis's theoretical construct provides a useful method for assessing an adversary's willingness to suffer costs and accept risks and thus

---

[56]Davis, *New Challenges for Defense Planning,* p. 209. On the subject of national ambition, see also Randall Schweller, *Deadly Imbalances* (New York: Columbia University Press, 1998).

[57]See also Huth, *Extended Deterrence and the Prevention of War,* p. 74. Huth notes "potential attackers seek quick and decisive results with the use of force at relatively low cost. It follows that the most effective military deterrent is the capacity of the defender to repulse an attack and deny the adversary its military objectives at the outset and early stages of an armed confrontation. The capabilities of the defender and its protégé to prevail in a prolonged struggle are not an effective deterrent because the potential attacker does not initiate the use of force with the intention to engage in a war of attrition. Deterrence based on the threat of denial is much more effective than the threat of punishment in a protracted war."

[58]Davis, *New Challenges for Defense Planning,* pp. 209–212. Davis's model is most applicable to state actors, but it can also provide useful insights into nonstate actors as well, e.g., the leadership of the Kosovo Liberation Army and its aspirations in the Balkans or the willingness of Osama bin Laden to continue his campaign of terrorism.

provides a basis for crafting a coercion regime to modify his potential or actual behavior.[59] In short, accurately understanding your adversary's motivation will give you a better appreciation for his perceived stake in the issue at hand—and an indication of the probable level of effort needed to coerce him. Sun Tzu's advice that "The prosecution of military affairs lies in according with and [learning] in detail the enemy's intentions" still merits attention.[60]

The second key element in beginning to craft a coercion strategy is an assessment of the adversary's capabilities—i.e., his means to achieve his aims and to resist your coercive efforts. This should include both quantitative and qualitative analyses of his capabilities in the four military operational domains (ground, sea, air, and space), as well as his infrastructure and population, to achieve his aims and resist coercion—and his centers of gravity or vulnerabilities in each of these areas.

Table 2.1 depicts a matrix that incorporates the dimensions of adversary will and capability. This matrix provides a simple framework for estimating the level of effort likely required for a successful coercion strategy and the basis for the military dimension of the net assessment that will determine the joint or coalition force packages necessary to achieve it.

Categorizing the Adversary's Coercion Threshold

Column A of Table 2.1 represents the normal peacetime relations among nations where there is little, if any, threat of military aggression, even though the "adversary"—or, perhaps more appropriately, the "competitor"—might possess significant military capabilities. Thus, competition is largely confined to the diplomatic, economic, and information realms, and such cases will not be discussed further here. Entries in Columns B through E, however, represent the cases

---

[59]It also has value for analyzing one's own mind-set or those of allies and other third parties.

[60]Ralph D. Sawyer, translator, *The Seven Military Classics of Ancient China* (Boulder, Colo.: Westview Press, 1993), p. 182.

Table 2.1

Assessment Matrix—Adversary Will and Capabilities

	Coercion Threshold vis-à-vis the Issue at Stake				
Relative Capabilities Possessed by the Adversary	A Responds to Nonmilitary Means (Economic, Diplomatic, Information)	B Coercion Requires Modest Military Means (Show of Force)	C Coercion Requires Physical Presence of Substantial Military Means	D Coercion Requires Application of Substantial Military Force	E Not Coercible— Must Be Defeated by Military Means
1 Negligible	A1	B1	C1	D1	E1
2 Modest	A2	B2	C2	D2	E2
3 Intermediate	A3	B3	C3	D3	E3
4 Substantial	A4	B4	C4	D4	E4

where military capability is potentially a necessary component of a coercive strategy (usually in concert with some or all of the other elements of power as well).

Adversaries in Column B are sufficiently committed to achieving their objectives that purely nonmilitary coercive pressure will not cause them to comply. However, a relatively minor show of force or other military threat may do so. This is often the case in peacekeeping operations, for example. Typically, actors in this category are unwilling to risk armed conflict at any level in pursuit of their goals, either because the stakes do not appear high enough or because they are highly averse to the risks entailed in military confrontation. In Column C are states against whom significant military means must be brought to bear to coerce—typically capabilities sufficient to defeat the enemy in the event of conflict. Coercion may require little or no actual use of force if the capability is clear, but the adversary must face the prospect of substantial costs before it will choose to comply. This was the level of commitment that many Western leaders attributed to Slobodan Milosevic prior to the 1999 bombing of Serbia, when President Bill Clinton and others expected that a few days of token air attacks would be sufficient to make Milosevic agree to the terms of the Rambouillet agreement.[61]

In fact, it turned out that Serbian commitment to resisting NATO's demands actually fell into Column D: cases where very substantial military force must be brought to bear, to the point of threatening the survival of the enemy state or regime, in order to achieve coercion. Faced with the prospect of such dire costs, even vital interests may appear to be worth sacrificing, but, unless the adversary is extremely weak, as in Haiti, this will likely require great effort on the part of the coercer. Finally, the cases in Column E are those in which the coercer is demanding that the target state or leader give up what it holds most dear, typically national survival or the political or personal survival of the enemy leaders. If in these cases, as in the Soviet effort to subdue Afghanistan or the U.S. effort to arrest Manuel Noriega, compliance will never be more attractive than resistance for the enemy, so victories will only be achieved through brute force.

Columns B, C, and D represent domains where an adversary can plausibly be coerced. Actually coercing him, however, depends on developing and applying a strategy that communicates your capability to prevail (based on an assessment of his capability [rows 1–4]), and your commitment (political will) to do so. Column E represents a domain where the extreme determination of the adversary makes a successful deterrence or compellence strategy essentially unachievable. In these cases, the adversary will have to be physically defeated to impose your will on him.

Assessing an Adversary's Capabilities to Resist Military Coercion

In the Table 2.1 matrix, we have arbitrarily classified adversary capabilities relative to those of the United States in four broad categories: negligible, modest, intermediate, and significant. For the purposes of this study, we have used the following definitions for these categories, focusing on the categories in Columns B through E that require military action as a component of a coercive strategy.

---

[61]See Wesley K. Clark, *Waging Modern War: Bosnia, Kosovo, and the Future of Combat* (New York: PublicAffairs, 2001), and Hosmer, *The Conflict over Kosovo.*

- **Negligible:** The potential adversary, although possibly capable of resisting diplomatic, economic, and informational coercion, does not have the capability to resist the application of military force and, if not coerced, can usually be defeated through a strike.[62] An example of an adversary in this category is Grenada during Operation Urgent Fury. Another example of a case where the adversary has negligible capability is the ongoing peacekeeping operation in Kosovo, where violence between poorly armed Serb and Albanian Kosovars has largely been deterred by lightly armed KFOR peacekeepers.

- **Modest:** The potential adversary has sufficient capabilities to require the application of low-level SSC military effort to defeat him if coercion failed. An example of this is the fielded forces of the Bosnian Serb Army, who conceded to NATO's coercive demands, embodied in the 1995 Dayton Accords, only after air strikes and battlefield defeats by their Croat and Bosnian enemies.

- **Intermediate:** The potential adversary has capabilities that would require the application of high-level SSC military effort to defeat him if deterrence failed. An example of this type of capability is Serbia during Operation Allied Force.

- **Significant:** The potential adversary has capabilities that would require the application of MTW-level effort to defeat him if deterrence failed. An example of this level of capability is North Korea.

In addition to assessing what level of capability a potential adversary possesses, one should identify centers of gravity and key vulnerabili-

---

[62]See Joint Chiefs of Staff, *Joint Publication 3-07: Joint Doctrine for Military Operations Other Than War* (Washington, D.C., 1995), III-15, for the following definition of strikes and raids: "**Strikes are offensive operations conducted to inflict damage on, seize, or destroy an objective for political purposes.** Strikes may be used for punishing offending nations or groups, upholding international law, or preventing those nations or groups from launching their own offensive actions. **A raid is usually a small-scale operation** involving swift penetration of hostile territory to secure information, confuse the enemy, or destroy installations. It ends with a planned withdrawal upon completion of the assigned mission. An **example of a strike** is Operation URGENT FURY, conducted on the island of Grenada in 1983. An **example of a raid** is Operation EL DORADO CANYON conducted against Libya in 1986, in response to the terrorist bombing of US Service members in Berlin." (Emphasis in the original.)

ties. For example, Operation Allied Force took advantage of the ability of NATO air power to operate with virtual impunity from high altitude against Serbian targets—a Serbian vulnerability. Finally, strategists should also consider whether adversaries possess asymmetric capabilities for countercoercion that are not captured in a purely quantitative assessment of military strength. For example, regardless of what other capabilities a potential adversary may possess, having the ability to strike the U.S. homeland or allies with nuclear or biological weapons could fundamentally alter the net assessment calculus for the United States.

Insights from a Matrixed View of Potential Adversaries

Combining the assessments of a potential adversary's coercion threshold and of his capabilities yields a perspective that gives a better indication of what an adversary will do and what will be necessary to deter or defeat him than can be derived from a simple comparison of military capabilities alone. This is particularly important in deterrence because the relative military strength of a potential adversary is not necessarily an accurate predictor of his propensity to commit aggression.[63] Still, "size does matter," and the most difficult deterrence cases are in the domains where the United States faces an implacable foe that cannot be dealt with in a rapid manner. This inability can be caused by a number of factors. First, as in the Soviet intervention in Afghanistan (E2), the adversary (the mujahideen), although possessing only modest military means, may be difficult to defeat because of complex terrain, external support, their commitment to protracted guerrilla warfare, and the absence of a center of gravity vulnerable to the means employed by the coercer. Second, as in the U.S. involvement in Vietnam (E3), the adversary (North Vietnam) may be willing to bear more pain than the coercer can or will inflict on him because of his commitment to nationalism, access to external support, and the availability of sanctuary from the coercer's capabilities—coupled with U.S. concerns of involving other actors (principally China in this case) in the conflict. Third, the scale of the effort required because of an adversary's (Iraq's) capabilities, as in Operation Desert Storm (D4), may require a substantial buildup of

---

[63]Huth, *Standing Your Ground*, pp. 103–149, 182.

forces and protracted "softening-up" before an attack is launched, thus precluding a quick result.

What is important about the E2, E3, and E4 cases is that misreading the will of an adversary—even if one has an accurate assessment of his capabilities—can result in an "undeterrable" or "uncompellable" conflict, one that requires far greater capabilities and resources to resolve than one would expect from a purely capabilities-based assessment. Various U.S. agencies have been successful—and are becoming more so—in the process of quantitative and qualitative assessment of the military capabilities of potential adversaries. Nevertheless, as will be shown in the case studies, there has often been considerably less success in assessing adversaries' intent and consequently the amount of force necessary to cause their accession to coercive demands.

As this discussion suggests, the matrix is intended to serve as a cognitive tool for strategy-making, not as a device for generating specific coercion strategies or force-sizing prescriptions.[64] Because coercion is a political process, its results depend to a significant degree on variables that defy quantitative measurement. Moreover, so many factors affect coercion outcomes that even if all those that were important in past cases could somehow be quantified, it would still be impossible to insert them into a deterministic model capable of producing consistently accurate predictions and reliable policy prescriptions for future situations.[65] Of course, historical experience still has much useful guidance to offer policymakers, but it means that searching for simple algorithms to tell the strategist exactly what sort or how many forces to employ in a particular coercive effort will be

---

[64]This is reflected by the fact that the columns refer to will, not merely to the value the enemy places on the issue in dispute. A state in cell D1 presumably cares more about the stakes than one in D4 because it has a comparable will to resist in spite of being far weaker.

[65]Political scientists have systematically applied quantitative methods to the study of deterrence and war since the 1960s, and, although some of their findings have been important, this enterprise has consistently been hampered not only by problems of measurement but also by the fundamental limitations inherent in using overly simple methods to analyze highly complex events. The results of this scholarly effort have fallen far short of the hopes of those who originally launched it. For an overview, see Jack Levy, "Quantitative Studies of Deterrence Success and Failure," in Paul C. Stern, Robert Axelrod, Robert Jervis, and Roy Radner, eds., *Perspectives on Deterrence* (New York: Oxford University Press, 1989).

fruitless.[66] In short, the practice of coercion, like the practice of war, remains as much an art as it is a science.[67]

---

[66]See Watts, "Ignoring Reality," and the response in Pape, "The Air Force Strikes Back."

[67]See Bernard Brodie, "Strategy as a Science," *World Politics*, Vol. 1, No. 4 (July 1949), pp. 467–488 and *War and Politics* (New York: Macmillan, 1973), Chapter 10.

Chapter Three

CASE STUDY RESULTS

To explore the application of the principles described in Chapter Two, we examined U.S. and foreign coercion cases in four categories along the spectrum of conflict: SASO, SSCs, MTWs, and strikes and raids. Within these categories, we focused on military operations that have an important coercive dimension, as shown below:[1]

- **SASO:** peace enforcement and peacekeeping operations that involve restoring stability through the deterrence of violence or the compellence of parties to comply with the underlying agreements supporting the operations.

- **SSC:** coercion of an adversary whose capabilities and will require significantly less effort than an MTW. We also include an example of a peace enforcement operation designed to deter the outbreak of conflict between Egypt and Israel (MFO [Multinational Force and Observers] Sinai).

- **MTW:** coercion of an adversary whose capabilities and will require substantial military effort to overcome—e.g., Operations Desert Shield and Desert Storm.

---

[1]We also examined a fifth category of the coercive use of military force—"support to civil authorities" (SCA)—and have included three such cases in the Appendix. We do not, however, discuss this category in the main body of the report because we believe that federal military forces, while often important, are complementary to domestic law enforcement and not central to the coercive effort in SCA. Clearly, however, much work needs to be done in the wake of recent events to better understand the role of federal military forces in homeland security—work that falls beyond the scope of this report.

- **Strikes** and **Raids:** military operations executed rapidly against adversaries with little capacity to resist, designed to achieve results directly, that may or may not also have a coercive effect.

The case studies are intended to place the theoretical principles of coercion in historical context. They are therefore primarily illustrative and are not intended to be in-depth assessments; neither are they "tests" of the core theory of coercion. Nevertheless, by studying a range of historical cases, even at such a basic level, it is possible to highlight factors that contribute prominently to the outcome of coercive strategies and to offer insights about success or failure and the relative utility of the types of military forces involved.

Two overarching criteria were used to select the cases studied here. First, the project required that cases span the full spectrum of military operations in which coercion is a viable strategy. Second, the study needed to examine both successes and failures of coercion. In addition, to be as comprehensive as possible, cases of both deterrence and compellence within each category of the spectrum of operations were included, and, wherever possible, cases were chosen that varied widely in other respects as well.[2]

To narrow the case list to a manageable size, several additional factors were considered. More-recent cases, particularly those occurring since the end of the Cold War, were preferred over earlier cases because of their closer relationship to today's geostrategic environment and state of military affairs. Fifteen of the 30 cases ultimately selected have occurred since 1990, and none of them predates the Korean War. Given the project's focus on assessing the coercive utility of different military forces, cases in which the military role was

---

[2] Several historical databases were used in the early stages of the case selection process. The *Correlates of War* database, maintained by the University of Michigan, includes data covering more than 1,000 conflicts from 1816 to 1992. The *International Crisis Behavior Project*, started by John Wilkenfeld and Michael Brecher, includes almost 900 records describing conflicts from 1918 to 1994. Both of these resources proved useful in the early stages of this project by providing a comprehensive universe of cases, chronologies, and geographical information. However, as the required level of detail increased, the databases proved too general to be of further use. Paul K. Huth's *Cases of Attempted Extended Deterrence* catalogs 58 selected cases of deterrence between 1885 and 1983. Because this database was more germane to the subject of the report, it proved to be of greater help in identifying and describing cases of interest.

prominent and well documented were preferred over those in which the military played a minor or uncertain role, and this aspect of the cases is emphasized in the analysis. However, in every instance, the military element complemented a larger strategic effort aimed at achieving the ultimate goal: the successful deterrence of aggression or the redress of aggressive behavior. Finally, because this report is designed primarily to assist U.S. strategists, cases involving the United States dominate the selections. However, a number of cases in which other states were the coercers are examined as well.

One result of applying these nonrandom selection criteria to the universe of possible cases is that the study cannot be used for statistical analysis. For example, the balance between success and failure in the cases presented here should not lead one to conclude that, statistically, a coercive strategy is as likely to succeed as it is to fail. Neither should one conclude that opportunities for coercion are distributed evenly across the spectrum of operations.

Instead, the cases provide a qualitative database for exploring the role of military forces in past coercive strategies. By studying its history, the factors contributing to the success or failure of an operation can be distilled and, after comparison with other operations conducted within and outside that area of the spectrum, an array of common characteristics emerge. It is our hope that by studying these characteristics, military planners at both the tactical and strategic level will have a tool to help them design the most effective possible forces and strategies for deterring or compelling aggressors. The following sections present the findings from the cases, focusing on the coercive potential of military forces, grouped according to where they fall along the spectrum of operations. For readers who desire additional historical details about these operations, a narrative description of each case appears in the Appendix, along with citations of historical sources in which further information can be found.

STABILITY AND SUPPORT OPERATIONS

Case Analyses

When a nation's internal security problems exceed the government's ability to address them domestically, a frequent product of deteriorating regimes, the interested parties may agree to a third-party intervention to preserve order. These operations, classified here as SASO, depend on permissive entry conditions and a secure environment in order to succeed in their effort to maintain and develop the rule of law. They often include both a compellence phase, during which the conditions for a lasting peace are firmly established, and a deterrence phase, during which stability is maintained and reinforced. This pattern appears in each of the three cases discussed here: NATO peace operations in Bosnia, including UNPROFOR, IFOR, and SFOR; humanitarian operations in Somalia, including Operation Provide Relief, Operation Restore Hope, and Operation Continue Hope; and Operation Joint Guardian in Kosovo.[3]

In each of these cases a premium was placed on force protection in order to minimize the costs of intervention for the coercer and to minimize the adversary's prospects for countercoercion. Force protection can be understood as a function of the rules of engagement (assuming the military capability to act on them), presence, and the threat of armed opposition. As reflected in these cases, SASO are typically distinguished from more-limited paramilitary operations or SCA missions by large areas of responsibility and the threat of armed opposition. The cases show that under these conditions the dynamic between troop presence and force protection often becomes central to the success or failure of the mission, particularly because SASO often only involve secondary or peripheral interests for the coercer.

As demonstrated by these cases, a direct relationship exists among the size of the theater, the size of the deployment, and troop protection. In the Bosnian operations, the intervention forces were charged with protecting the population and disarming belligerent forces. The size of the area of operations (50,000 square miles) demanded a large force to achieve the level of presence necessary both to impose order and to defend against attack. The lightly armed UNPROFOR accommodated to the demands of force protection by concentrating their deployment of 40,000 peacekeepers in and around the six UN-designated "safe areas." However, this arrangement forfeited any ability to control sources of violence elsewhere in Bosnia. As shown in the subsequent operation, IFOR, this problem

---

[3]The phase preceding Operation Joint Guardian—Operation Allied Force—is categorized in this report as an SSC and will be examined in the next section.

might have been addressed by deploying a similar number of more heavily armed troops with more-robust rules of engagement throughout the area of operations, had the United Nations and the nations providing the peacekeeping forces been willing to undertake such a mission. In the current phase of Bosnian peacekeeping, SFOR, the number of troops has been reduced. This drawdown was made possible by a reduction of the threat level, while the area of responsibility remained the same. To accomplish the mission with fewer troops, planners retained robust rules of engagement and provided the force with adequate mobility to respond quickly to threats throughout the area of operations.

During operations in Somalia, planners initially miscalculated the role of presence in ensuring stability and accomplishing mission objectives. The first force deployed to the country, Operation Provide Relief (UNOSOM I), initially consisted of only 50 unarmed observers. Despite being reinforced twice and ultimately amounting to 4,269 troops and observers centered in the capital of Mogadishu, the dimensions of the crisis, and of the disintegrating 250,000-square-mile country, dwarfed UNOSOM I. The international community responded with a more robust effort named Operation Restore Hope (UNITAF), which began in December 1992 and eventually deployed 38,000 troops including 28,000 from the United States. The UN mandate for Operation Restore Hope included two important missions: the provision of humanitarian assistance to the Somali people and the restoration of order in southern Somalia. In contrast to the later UN deployment to Bosnia, limiting presence to a few designated "safe areas" was not an option because the mission called for the distribution of assistance throughout the country. To meet their mission, Army planners focused their initial efforts on building bridges and 1,100 kilometers of roads and providing intra-theater communications.[4] These structural improvements and the

---

[4]Kenneth Allard, *Somalia Operations: Lessons Learned* (Washington, D.C.: National Defense University Press, 1995), pp. 15–18, 77–82. Communications proved particularly difficult for Army units in Somalia because units commonly operated at distances greater than the range of their tactical FM radios and Mobile Subscriber Equipment. To maintain communication links, Army forces in Somalia had to rely on the very limited number of HF and TACSAT systems available to the force. The commercial INMARSAT system enabled communications between coalition forces and nongovernmental organizations.

use of air assault forces permitted the rapid deployment of troops when specific threats arose while also contributing to the distribution of humanitarian aid. The Army further magnified its effective presence by concentrating limited resources on defending high-value targets, such as aid convoys. This strategy, often requiring the dispersal of troops across wide areas, was made possible by the relatively stable security environment and by rules of engagement that preserved impartiality and good relations with the population. Striking this delicate balance between force-protection demands and deploying a limited number of troops through a large area proved essential to the success of Restore Hope.

The emergence of armed opposition greatly increased force protection demands during the final phase of operations in Somalia, Operation Continue Hope (UNOSOM II). The transition to UNO-SOM II resulted in a new mission objective: to disarm Somalis regardless of the threat they posed to the peacekeepers. This mission threatened the power base of several Somali factions and increased the resistance directed against UNOSOM II troops, who were now seen as active players in the ongoing struggle for power. The expanded mission and increased threat level demanded an increased presence in the region. However, UNOSOM II forces totaled only 28,000 troops and the U.S. contribution fell to 4,500 Quick Reaction soldiers complemented by Task Force Ranger. To accomplish the mission, the UN commander issued rules of engagement permitting troops to engage armed Somalis without provocation. Rather than increase the security of the peacekeepers, this directive directly contributed to an escalation in violence and the need for still greater force protection.[5]

Events in Somalia began to unravel in June 1993, when 24 Pakistani soldiers were killed in an ambush. The UN passed a resolution calling for the apprehension of those responsible. On October 2, Task Force Ranger conducted a raid, whose purpose was the capture of Somali warlord Mohammed Farah Aideed, believed to be responsible for the ambush of the Pakistani soldiers. In the ensuing "Battle of Mogadishu," 18 American soldiers died and 75 were wounded. In the aftermath of the action, the United States made the decision to with-

---

[5]Allard, *Somalia Operations,* pp. 18–20, 35–38.

draw from Somalia. In preparation for the withdrawal, UNOSOM II was reinforced and the planners adapted their tactics and mission objectives to emphasize force protection. The UN experience in Somalia shows the importance of realistically gauging threat levels in order to deploy forces capable of meeting mission objectives. The dimensions of the problem in physical and sociological terms seem to have deceived planners at the opening and closing stages of the crisis, ultimately leading to the overextension of a force lacking the strength and capability to perform its assigned tasks.

UNPROFOR's deployment to Bosnia-Herzegovina shared its central mission with UNOSOM II, the partial disarmament of the local population. Although this task was an ambitious compellence mission in that it demanded a major change in the status quo, UNPROFOR possessed insufficient strength to impose its will. Indeed, the force had insufficient military capability even to defend itself, much less protect the population from concerted attack. These shortcomings derived primarily from an unrealistic assessment by UN force planners of the threat posed by the Bosnian Serb Army. To successfully implement a coercive strategy at this point on the spectrum, a military force must possess an unambiguous capability to control opposing forces.[6] The only capability provided to UNPROFOR that might have deterred a Serbian attack was the threat of NATO air strikes. Both military commanders and political leaders undermined the value of this threat by stating a disinclination to employ air power, and in isolated cases when air strikes were used, by giving the Bosnian Serb Army prior warning. The weakness of UNPROFOR, already understood by Serb commanders, became widely apparent when peacekeepers came under pressure. Lacking the military capability to defend themselves, caused and compounded by a political unwillingness to deploy in strength and provide adequate fire support, UNPROFOR troops were forced to surrender, taken hostage and rendered helpless as Serb troops freely violated designated "safe

---

[6]Although theory suggests that a coercive strategy can succeed by punishing or threatening to punish an adversary, the case studies suggest that punishment is often not practical at lower levels of conflict. Rather than compel belligerents to comply with demands by inflicting pain until they do so, successful coercive strategies at the SASO level may be better served by working to establish direct control over target populations, coercing through classic deterrence by denial.

areas."[7] The limited threat at this level of the spectrum allows the coercer, provided the political will exists, to deploy forces possessed of incontestable strength. The case histories suggest the resulting capability for deterrence or compellence by denial contributes greatly to the success of such missions.

Force Structure Implications of SASO

The central challenge of SASO is the need to establish a ground-force presence throughout a large area while maintaining an uncontestable level of force protection.[8] Pervasive presence maximizes the intervention force's coercive power, while force protection limits the adversary's ability to mount punitive attacks of his own. Although increasing troop mobility allows forces to expand their range to respond to threats as they arise, this approach worked only in relatively low-threat environments. During the opening stages of an operation against potentially significant opposition, the cases strongly support large-scale deployment of ground troops. If security conditions later improve, this raises the likelihood that the number of troops can be safely reduced.

The nature of the troop presence must be appropriate to the security threat posed by potential adversaries. However, these adversaries will not always be immediately apparent during the planning of an operation, which suggests a need for constant reassessment of the true security environment. In general, it seems sufficient to deploy a force capable of defeating any other force or coalition of forces in the theater, but this may not always be a feasible option. The dangers of attempting to coerce an enemy from a position of weakness were vividly demonstrated during UNPROFOR. Increasing force strength,

---

[7]Kofi Annan, *Report of the Secretary-General Pursuant to General Assembly Resolution 53/35: The Fall of Srebrenica* (New York: United Nations, 1999), pp. 105–107.

[8]See James T. Quinlivan, "Flexible Ground Forces," in Williams, *Holding the Line*, p. 187. Quinlivan attempts to answer the question of the force requirement for SASO by comparing the ratio of peacekeepers to population as that of policemen in a civil society. In the United States, this ratio is two police officers per thousand population. In SASO cases that have required intervention, the ratio has been approximately 20 per thousand (IFOR in Bosnia; KFOR in Kosovo). He also notes that as a specific situation stabilizes over time, the ratio decreases, e.g., SFOR in Bosnia has a ratio of roughly 10 per thousand.

whether through issuing robust rules of engagement or deploying more-heavily-armored forces, may increase coercive power. The former will enhance the adversary's perceptions of threat credibility, while the latter makes the coercer's military capability more intimidating, and both may contribute to presence by allowing for the wider dispersal of better-protected forces.

The SASO mission is accomplished primarily through troop presence, making land forces dominant within it, but the force application role of the other services can be important, both for generating the abstract threat of punitive strikes and, in extreme situations, providing the necessary firepower to protect deployed forces from attack. In the two cases above where air support was employed, Somalia and UNPROFOR, this tool was not employed with great effectiveness. In Somalia, the escalation represented by the use of attack helicopters and AC-130 gunships in the pursuit of General Aideed worsened the security environment by aggravating the local population. The failure of commanders to use air power at crucial moments in support of UNPROFOR is well documented but illustrates the unwillingness to employ force that seems disproportionate to the mission of peacekeeping.[9] That analysis, founded on the illusion of a permissive environment, deprived UNPROFOR of the capability to defeat the Serb attack on Srebrenica. Had the ground force possessed the organic capability to defeat armored attack or had the commanders demonstrated a willingness to employ air forces to do so, the case analysis suggests that the Bosnian Serb Army would not have staged the assault, just as it was deterred from attacking forces deployed in IFOR and KFOR.

Finally, when establishing the rules of engagement for SASO, it is vital to remember that the primary goal of SASO is to reduce the level of violence. Just as recklessly employing air power would endanger ground troops, approving rules of engagement that provoke open ground combat can also lead to increased risk to the force and ultimately to the failure of the mission. If the security environment requires heavy firepower operating under highly permissive rules of engagement, then planners should reexamine the strategic situation and consider whether SASO is the appropriate response.

---

[9]Ibid., p. 107.

SMALLER-SCALE CONTINGENCIES

Case Analyses

SSCs present a greater challenge to decisionmakers attempting to coerce aggressors. In SASO, the threat of organized opposition exists at a low enough level for intervening forces to maintain order by directly controlling the population and potential aggressors. At the SSC level, however, forces must contend with the strength of nation-states or significant nonstate actors backed by both official and popular resolve to resist intervention. For this reason, it is at the level of SSCs that the opponent's disposition, including both his will and capability to resist, becomes crucial to the employment of coercive strategies. The SSCs examined in this study demonstrate these greater challenges. They are MFO Sinai, Operations Northern and Southern Watch, the British intervention in Kuwait in 1961, the defense of the Falkland Islands, Operation Restore Democracy in Haiti, the Russian campaigns in Chechnya, Operation Allied Force, and the superpower interventions in Afghanistan and Vietnam.

The three dominant characteristics of successful military strategies at the SSC level are correctly understanding the adversary's goals and his commitment to achieving them; deploying sufficient military capability to frustrate the adversary's objectives, whether aggressive or defensive; and the ability to isolate the opponent physically and politically. The complexity of SSCs is such that, even when these criteria are satisfied, success is not ensured. Failure is never a trivial prospect, but all the more so at this level of the spectrum, where it usually entails both substantial casualties and the abandonment of significant national interests.

Before pursuing a strategy of military coercion, it is important to determine whether such a strategy has any chance of success. At the SSC level, with the emergence of a capable and well-organized opposition and reduced prospects of directly controlling the population, a military force's role in coercion lies in its ability to threaten and inflict punishment, denial, or both. In two of the cases studied here, U.S. operations in Vietnam and Soviet operations in Afghanistan, and possibly a third, the crisis in Chechnya, the willingness of the compelled party to withstand punishment exceeded the compeller's willingness or ability to inflict it. President Raul Cedras of

Haiti, on the other hand, was relatively easy to coerce during Operation Uphold Democracy, in which a credible threat of pain and inevitable defeat (and the offer of a reasonably attractive alternative if he complied) convinced him to change his behavior. While it is not always possible to tell how susceptible an opponent will be to military coercion, applying the guidelines in Chapter Two provides a general indication of the level of effort required to achieve your aims. If an adversary's will to persist exceeds the coercer's will to inflict pain, then pursuing a strategy of punitive military coercion will likely lead to failure. That said, it is important to note that a government's ability to achieve its goals through unfettered military escalation may be tempered by sensibility. On the other hand, by exploiting the increased lethality of conventional weapons while restricting media access to the theater, Russian forces in Chechnya are now achieving limited success against an adversary who appears relatively unsusceptible to coercion.

Having determined that military coercion is technically and politically feasible, it is necessary to design a force with sufficient capability to succeed. At this point it serves to distinguish between deterrence and compellence while accepting that many cases contain elements of both and may shift between the two. The case studies suggest that to successfully deter an adversary it is often necessary to deploy a force capable of defeating a concerted attack in order to convey credibility and hedge against the many intangibles that can contribute to deterrence failure despite an adequate defense. This level of deterrence has been achieved in Operations Northern and Southern Watch, which have successfully deterred major Iraqi violations of the no-fly zones for many years. The uncontestable superiority of Allied air forces has convinced the Iraqi regime to abandon direct challenges to the operations by violating the no-fly zones, though they continue to shoot at planes enforcing the mission, thereby marginally raising the cost of deterrence. The success of other cases, such as the British defense of Kuwait in 1961 and the MFO Sinai, presents more-ambiguous evidence about the role of military forces in preserving the status quo. The MFO Sinai in particular presents a quandary because the force, while certainly contributing to the stability of the region, is utterly incapable of confronting an attack from either party. Likewise, the MFO's function as a trip wire is obviated by its limited mobility and presence. An

attacking force could avoid engaging the MFO Sinai by simply cir-
cumventing it.

The case of unsuccessful deterrence of an SSC studied here, Britain's
failure to deter Argentine forces from invading the Falkland Islands
in 1982, illustrates what can happens when the international relationship crumbles and a state attempts to achieve its goals through
military means, believing that it is capable of doing so and can
escape excessively costly retaliation. Prior to the invasion, Britain
garrisoned the Falklands with a small force of approximately 40 Royal
Marines. Although it would have been difficult to maintain a ground
force capable of repelling a full-scale invasion by Argentina on the
remote island group, or even to maintain the necessary naval forces
offshore, a consistent policy of declaring commitment to the Falklands' defense and maintaining a force capable of a significant
defense would have contributed greatly to deterrence. Furthermore,
had the British government correctly understood the pressure felt by
the Argentine junta to generate a military victory for domestic political reasons and had they reacted forcefully to previous incidents
suggesting a rise in Argentine nationalism toward the islands, it is
possible that a simple reinforcement would have communicated the
necessary commitment to Buenos Aires.

Compellence missions, those in which the objective is to change an
adversary's current behavior, generally require a more overt demon-
stration of capability and commitment, often including the discriminate application of force. Although there is one case in this set,
Operation Restore Democracy, in which the threat of force alone
compelled an adversary, the other cases examined here indicate that
successful compellence at the SSC level often requires a liberal, and
sometimes drastic, application of force. During Operation Allied
Force, the Serbian leadership in Belgrade decided to end the bombing campaign by agreeing to withdraw from Kosovo and allow NATO
peacekeepers to occupy the province. This decision was influenced
in large part by diminishing public support for the regime, the result
of intense targeting of dual-use infrastructure targets, such as electric
power plants, which stressed both the economy and popular support
for the war.[10] The second phase, named Operation Joint Guardian,

---

[10]Hosmer, *The Conflict over Kosovo.*

deterred aggression between the Kosovo Liberation Army and the Serbian Army while protecting the population from unorganized social unrest.

Early in the Algerian Civil War, the French successfully compelled insurgents to stop crossing border areas by setting up an elaborate system of frontier defenses. While this system existed, from 1957 to 1958, external support for the Algerian rebels was reduced by 90 percent, significantly increasing their vulnerability to French counter-insurgency operations.[11] Compared with the discriminate use of air power in Kosovo, the French method appears crude, but at the time it was heralded as a remarkable advance in warfighting. The common aspect of these two examples is that they directly addressed the factors enabling resistance, demonstrating the importance of identifying and targeting the assets your adversary needs to continue to struggle.

In each of these cases, the ability to isolate the adversary in either the political or physical dimension accompanied a successful outcome. The agreement reached during Operation Allied Force to include Russia in a subsequent peacekeeping force, for instance, not only deprived Serbia of a potential ally but also had the added benefit of making the prospect of the intervention less threatening, thus lowering the expected costs of compliance with NATO's demands.[12] Coalition-building, though it affects military strategy, is primarily a diplomatic tool and was used as such in Restore Democracy, Northern and Southern Watch, Kuwait in 1961, and Allied Force. An alternative to coalition-building is to obstruct the adversary's attempts to establish contacts with outside supporters. This was the method used by Russia in the second Chechen campaign after the campaign of 1996 provoked international criticism. By restricting media access and the movement of Chechen diplomats, the Russians effectively isolated the conflict, disheartening their adversary and freeing their hands to employ severe tactics.[13]

---

[11]Peter Brush, "The Story Behind the McNamara Line," *Vietnam*, No. 2 (February 1996), pp. 18–24.

[12]Michael R. Gordon, "Crisis in the Balkans: Russia; Moscow Says Its Envoy Was a Key to Success," *New York Times*, June 4, 1999, p. A1.

[13]The Russian ability to isolate Chechnya from world media scrutiny seems to be weakening as their casualties mount and the conflict drags on.

Using military force to isolate an adversary is sometimes possible but usually requires a great deal of effort. The French effectively isolated Algeria by sealing its borders and controlling movement throughout the huge country with a series of checkpoints and active patrols. However, the effort required to maintain the Quadrillage, as the strategy came to be known, completely occupied tens of thousands of French soldiers and was abandoned after a year. During the Vietnam War, targeting the sanctuary countries of Laos and Cambodia was frequently cited as the key to victory in South Vietnam. The military employed both air and land forces to interdict supply routes and attack Vietnamese forces in these countries. Fundamental errors in determining the susceptibility of the enemy to coercion, however, ultimately caused these costly efforts to fail to achieve their larger strategic goals.[14]

Force Structure Implications of SSCs

Because conflict at the SSC level anticipates a well-armed opposing force, any military deployment must possess robust defensive and offensive capabilities to accomplish its mission. The specific force mix deployed depends on the adversary's willingness to resist and its specific capabilities, the terrain, the availability of high-value targets, and the willingness of the coercer to escalate the conflict. This range of factors contributed to a wide range of forces being deployed in the cases studied here, though almost all were joint forces. Although the cases suggest that one-dimensional forces can successfully deter one-dimensional threats, in compellence missions it is useful to be able to adjust the threat and application of force according to your adversary's behavior, and coercive flexibility is enhanced by the capability to conduct operations in several dimensions—for example, threatening aerial bombardment or a ground invasion to achieve mission objectives.

In the MFO Sinai and Northern and Southern Watch, the coercive strategy was dominated by a single service, the Army and the Air Force, respectively. The Army is particularly well suited to long-term peacekeeping deployments, such as the MFO Sinai, because it com-

---

[14]Furthermore, North Vietnam was never completely isolated, politically or physically, from its sources of external support.

bines sustainability with the ability to conduct sustained local observation of ground forces in the region. In this case, the limited capacity of the single-service deployment can be seen as a benefit because it renders the force incapable of exceeding its mandate or posing a threat to either Israel or Egypt. Likewise, Operations Northern and Southern Watch are primarily single-service because their mission extends only to enforcing the no-fly zones, although the deployment of ground troops to these missions is necessary to provide base security

In more-challenging scenarios as represented by the majority of the cases studied here, the missions did call for joint deployments, particularly when the objective was to compel the adversary. One advantage conferred by joint forces was operational versatility. A good example of this is Operation Uphold Democracy. It was communicated to President Cedras that the 82nd Airborne Division troops en route to Haiti were prepared to fight when they arrived. Convinced, Cedras capitulated, and the same soldiers conducted an unopposed occupation. When the situation on the ground is uncertain or liable to change on short notice, the ability to deploy versatile assets to the theater holds great value. Ground forces distinguish themselves for their operational versatility, though had Cedras not capitulated, the soldiers of the 82nd Airborne would certainly have benefited from the presence and capability of joint fires.

Insofar as jointness is associated with increased capability, joint forces also help convey a message to the adversary: things could get worse. Successful compellence depends on the adversary considering the cost of compliance and comparing it with the cost of further resistance. Joint forces, even when they are not used, expand the coercer's escalatory options. Although it was never employed, the deployment of Task Force Hawk to Albania during Operation Allied Force, in conjunction with ground forces deployed along the Kosovo-Macedonia border and the Marine Expeditionary Unit (MEU) offshore, may have influenced Milosevic's decision to comply with NATO's demands by making the threat of an eventual NATO invasion of Serbia more tangible and credible.[15]

---

[15]The reasons for Milosevic's capitulation are still the subject of active controversy. See, for example, Hosmer, *The Conflict over Kosovo*, and Byman and Waxman, "Kosovo and the Great Air Power Debate."

Finally, deploying a flexible force anticipates future stages of the crisis. The great capacity of air and naval forces to apply long-range firepower may be essential in the opening stages of an operation when there is a high-risk environment created by an aggressive adversary. The ability to strike high-value targets with virtual impunity can be of great coercive value. If the adversary refuses to comply with the coercive demands, he may then find land forces more compelling because of their ability to seize and hold territory, which is often reason enough to include them in a force package. If the adversary does agree to the coercer's demands, then it is often necessary to deploy ground troops to secure and verify territorial or jurisdictional concessions. In the later stages of a successful mission, particularly if it transitions to something resembling a SASO, it is likely that ground forces will come to dominate. Even then, however, the availability of air and naval forces continues to provide valuable force protection and coercive leverage. In cases where maintaining the desired end-state will require capabilities different from those needed to attain it, the initial creation of a joint task force facilitates the transition while providing the framework for success.

The nature of the mission will indicate whether a joint or single-service deployment is appropriate, but other factors, such as target quality and the expected length of the mission, should also be considered when designing a force. Target quality refers to the availability and vulnerability of targets contributing to a regime's ability or willingness to resist. In some less-developed countries or when confronting certain nonstate actors, such targets may be difficult to identify or entirely nonexistent, greatly limiting the coercive value of naval or air power and leaving the job of military coercion almost entirely in the hands of ground forces because of their ability to occupy, to police, and in general to interact with local populations on a continuous, face-to-face basis.[16] On the other hand, even against less-than-modern and nonstate adversaries, appropriate intelligence and strategy may enable air or naval power to contribute substan-

---

[16]If what your adversary values most, or what his survival depends on, is an asset that is intrinsically difficult to target, religious identity for example, it will contribute greatly to his ability to resist military coercive strategies.

tially to military coercion by attacking important denial or punishment targets.[17]

A final consideration that affects force design at the SSC level should be the expected length of the operation. Although end-states and exit strategies are often much harder to foresee in reality than some strategists like to admit, analyzing your enemy's capability and commitment (Table 2.1) makes it possible to estimate the amount of coercive effort that will be required to succeed. The longer a force expects to be engaged, the greater the need for sustainability and logistics infrastructure. The Army possesses unique capabilities in this area, and these should be exploited. Furthermore, an initial Army presence provides the kernel for future reinforcements, a useful hedge against uncertainty and unanticipated mission demands.

MAJOR THEATER WARS

Case Analyses

The military plays the central role in coercive strategies at the MTW level. The case studies show that at the outset of an MTW the political will required to act decisively usually exists, primarily because a developing crisis threatens vital national interests, and this level of commitment facilitates coercive efforts. On the other hand, by definition the adversaries encountered at this level of conflict possess considerable resources of their own with which to resist and to coerce their enemies in turn, including powerful armed forces and strong allies that can complicate attempts to pressure them through political or economic isolation.

Neither of the two primary cases examined here represents absolute successes or failures of coercion for either actor. Rather, specific aspects of the two cases studied, the conflict on the Korean peninsula from 1950 to the present and the conflict with Iraq from 1990 to 1991, provide a variety of outcomes of coercive strategy at the MTW

---

[17]See, for example, Peter W. Gray, "The Myth of Air Control and the Realities of Imperial Policing," *Aerospace Power Journal*, Vol. 15, No. 3 (Fall 2001), pp. 21–31, and Wray R. Johnson, "Air Power and Restraint in Small Wars: Marine Corps Aviation in the Second Nicaraguan Campaign," *Aerospace Power Journal*, Vol. 15, No. 3 (Fall 2001), pp. 32–41.

level. Two other cases provide ambiguous, yet provocative, examples of deterrence at the MTW level. These are Operation Vigilant Warrior and the Chinese objections to a U.S. invasion of North Vietnam. While the first two cases rest primarily on a comparison of capability and will, the latter two are more complex, involving hidden intentions and ghosts from the past.

All conflict begins with an initial failure of deterrence. In the case of the Korean War, South Korea and the United States failed to deter an invasion from the North. Although several factors contributed to this event, certainly including the weakness of the South Korean Army compared with that of the North, U.S. statements prior to the invasion have drawn particular attention from historians. As part of a general military drawdown following World War II, the Truman administration declared its limited interests in Asia, explicitly excluding the Korean peninsula. The North Korean government, confident that its aggression would not provoke a response from America, welcomed this statement of noninterference and prepared for the invasion. At a later stage in the Korean War, as UN troops invaded the North and pushed toward the Yalu River, another failure of deterrence took place. Despite repeated warnings from China that it would not tolerate a UN invasion of North Korea, the UN Command (UNC) pressed on, eventually prompting the open involvement of China in the conflict and leading to a two-year stalemate. Had Chinese deterrent threats been less ambiguous, and had the Chinese military preparation for intervention been more visible, it is possible that the UNC would have yielded. Thus, both of these examples demonstrate the importance of clearly communicating demands and expectations in coercion, even if clarity comes at the expense of military operational secrecy.

Following the initial failure of deterrence in the Korean War, North Korean forces advanced rapidly down the peninsula. To confront the force and compel the North to halt the invasion and withdraw beyond the 38th parallel, a decision was made to deploy U.S. troops stationed in Japan. The centerpiece of this deployment was Task Force Smith, consisting of 500 ground troops with artillery support but no air or naval assets and largely ineffective antitank weapons. Paul Wolfowitz, now Deputy Secretary of Defense, once described the deployment as "too late to deter, too weak, too small, too ill-equipped and too ill-trained to defend, but large enough to die."[18] North Korea was not deterred, and Task Force Smith suffered heavy casualties. By responding with a small ground force that was difficult to protect and unsupported by air or naval forces, the planners demonstrated a total misapprehension of their adversary's will and capability. This aspect of the Korean War, and the deaths of American soldiers placed haplessly in harm's way, demonstrates the gravity of coercive strategy at the MTW level and the continued importance of force protection considerations despite imminent threats to national interests.

The aftermath of the Korean War created conditions for classic conventional deterrence. The 38th parallel became a highly fortified Demilitarized Zone, lined on both sides by minefields, artillery emplacements, and large armies. The threat these defenses posed to both sides and the geopolitical and escalatory constraints of the Cold War have allowed the stalemate to prevail since 1953 with only minor incursions from the North. As the South Korean economy and armed forces subsequently grew stronger, the United States was comfortable reducing its presence and gradually drew down the size of its force deployment to South Korea. Some observers argue that the South Korean Army is now strong enough to deter, and probably defeat, an invasion by an adversary weakened by corruption, famine, and political isolation and therefore advocate that the United States withdraw its remaining 36,000 troops stationed on the peninsula.[19] These analyses generally discount the argument that the U.S. troop presence is symbolically significant, signaling a clear commitment to South Korea, and that these troops project a stabilizing influence throughout East Asia.

A secondary case of coercion studied at the MTW level derived indirectly from the aftermath of hostilities on the Korean peninsula. During the Vietnam War, the Chinese government, as it had during

---

[18]Paul D. Wolfowitz, "Remarks to the Carnegie Council, June 27, 1990," available at http://www.fas.org/news/skorea/1990/900627-rok-usia.htm, accessed May 2, 2001.

[19]Michael O'Hanlon, "Stopping a North Korean Invasion: Why Defending South Korea Is Easier Than the Pentagon Thinks," *International Security*, Vol. 22, No. 4 (Spring 1998), pp. 135–176; Doug Bandow, "Leave Korea to the Koreans," available at http://www.cato.org//dailys/05-27-00.html, accessed May 2, 2001.

the UN intervention in Korea, opposed the presence of U.S. troops in Vietnam and supported the North Vietnamese government during its conflict with the South. U.S. government documents indicate that fear of China entering the war on North Vietnam's behalf contributed to the U.S. decision not to invade North Vietnam, and it also led to restrictions on the use of U.S. air power over the North.[20] This fear was driven in large part by the parallels between this conflict and the Korean War, particularly the role played by China.[21] Chinese leaders actively objected to the war in South Vietnam and made unambiguous statements regarding their interests in the North, and their deterrence strategy was greatly strengthened by a recent historical precedent that gave credibility to their threats.

The history of Iraq's confrontation with its neighbors and the Western world since 1990 reveals a variety of coercive strategies succeeding and failing by degrees. Like the Korean conflict, the history discussed here begins with a fateful misunderstanding. At a meeting held on July 25, 1990, U.S. Ambassador to Iraq April Glaspie reportedly told Saddam Hussein:

> We have no opinion on the Arab-Arab conflicts, like your border disagreement with Kuwait. I was in the American Embassy in Kuwait during the late 60's. The instruction we had during this period was that we should express no opinion on this issue and that the issue is not associated with America. James Baker has directed our official spokesmen to emphasize this instruction. . . . I received an instruction to ask you, in the spirit of friendship—not in the spirit of confrontation—regarding your intentions.[22]

It has been suggested that Ambassador Glaspie did not unambiguously express U.S. support for Kuwait and that this might have contributed to the failure of deterrence and the Iraqi decision to invade in early August. However, Richard Haass recognizes that Ambas-

---

[20]William C. Gibbons, *The U.S. Government and the Vietnam War: Executive and Legislative Roles and Relationships. Part IV: July 1965–January 1968* (Princeton, N.J.: Princeton University Press, 1995), pp. 102–107.

[21]See Yuen Foong Khong, *Analogies at War* (Princeton, N.J.: Princeton University Press, 1992).

[22]"Excerpts from Iraqi Document on Meeting with U.S. Envoy," *New York Times*, September 23, 1990.

sador Glaspie might have "jacked up her message 10 percent in terms of firmness" but attributes Iraq's aggression to broader psychological and historical causes:

> Saddam probably figured he could do it quickly, as he could militarily, and the Arab world and the world at large would bitch and moan for a couple of days, and then people would get used to it. And the world would essentially learn to live with it. And the United States, which had left Lebanon a decade before and so forth was not going to do anything.[23]

The initial U.S. deployment to the theater in August 1990 performed both a deterrent and a compellent mission. The ultimate strategic objective of the deployment, known as Operation Desert Shield, was to drive Iraqi forces from Kuwait. Even when coalition forces were vastly outnumbered in August, and before there was any approval to use force to achieve this objective, commanders still demanded that Iraq withdraw, although they understood this was not likely to succeed.[24] The more immediate mission of operation Desert Shield was to deter Iraqi forces from invading Saudi Arabia, particularly the ports that would be necessary for unloading follow-on forces. For this mission, the ready brigade of the 82nd Airborne Division and several Air Force fighter squadrons were deployed in the days following the invasion of Kuwait. Fortunately for the soldiers, Iraq did not invade Saudi Arabia. Neither is there any indication that this was ever its intention. Although it was a light force with low mobility and little offensive capability, the 82nd performed a vital function by instantly reassuring America's allies, adding weight to diplomatic initiatives in the UN, and creating a ground presence for future reinforcements to build on.

Following the initial deployment several steps were made to strengthen the coercive effort. First, Iraq was isolated by an economic embargo and the condemnation of Arab nations from whom Saddam Hussein might have expected assistance. Second, the force

---

[23]Richard Haass, PBS "Frontline" interview (original airdate), January 9, 1996, at http://www.pbs.org/wgbh/pages/frontline/gulf/oral/haass/1.html, accessed May 2, 2001.

[24]Dick Cheney, PBS "Frontline" interview (original airdate), January 9, 1996, at http://www.pbs.org/wgbh/pages/frontline/gulf/oral/cheney/1.html, accessed May 5, 2001.

was strengthened, first to a level capable of defending Saudi Arabia, then to a level more than sufficient for attacking and defeating Iraqi forces. As then–Secretary of Defense Dick Cheney recalled later:

> In August all we had over there initially was the ready brigade of the 82nd Airborne and wing of F-15s from Langley [AFB] in Virginia and relatively small forces at the outset, so it wasn't really until the end of August that we began to feel fairly comfortable with the size forces we were getting there. That we could respond aggressively if he were to launch an attack. In September, as you move through the month of September and U.S. forces have arrived, the 24th from Fort Jackson the other kinds of heavy forces began to flow into the region, elements of the 101st, the Marines and so forth and then you begin to feel that you've achieved your first stage objective which is to be able to defend Saudi Arabia. Then you move into the second phase, which is, OK—now what are we going to do to get this guy out of Kuwait?[25]

The hope was that the combination of economic and diplomatic isolation, reinforced by a threat to destroy both his military and economic infrastructure, would prove sufficient to persuade Saddam Hussein to abandon Kuwait. However, a strong commitment to resist, perhaps fortified by doubting the coalition's political will to proceed, led the Iraqi regime to refuse all demands regardless of the strength of the opposing force or the hardships endured or threatened, until the coalition air and ground offensive in early 1991 drove Iraqi forces from Kuwait.

In addition to the main coercive effort, the United States and its allies also faced the threat that Iraq would employ chemical, biological, or even nuclear weapons. It was known that Iraq possessed chemical and biological agents and had used the former in past conflicts against Iran and the Iraqi Kurdish population. While these weapons are of limited utility in desert environments and the coalition troops were well prepared to deal with them—probably far better prepared than their Iraqi counterparts—the danger was real and demanded a response. The United States communicated to Iraq that "in the event of a first use of a weapon of mass destruction by Iraq, the United States reserved the right to use *any* form of retaliation (presum-

---

[25]Ibid.

ably up to and including nuclear weapons),"[26] and similar threats were issued by the United Kingdom and Israel. Again, whether Iraq actually intended to employ unconventional weapons is unknown. What can be said is that Iraq had the capability to use WMD but chose not to do so. Against a larger unsuccessful effort to compel Iraq to withdraw from Kuwait without using force, this success in deterring the use of unconventional weapons stands out.

The survival of Saddam Hussein's regime at the conclusion of Operation Desert Storm necessitated subsequent missions to coerce the damaged but unvanquished Iraqi military. Chief among these efforts were Operations Northern and Southern Watch, discussed in the previous section, and Operation Vigilant Warrior. Operation Vigilant Warrior responded to events similar to those of 1961, when the British reinforced the Kuwaiti border in the face of what appeared to be an imminent Iraqi invasion. In 1994, the United States responded in strength to provocative mobilizations inside Iraq, rapidly fielding a brigade of armor that had been prepositioned in the theater and deploying large numbers of aircraft. Although Iraq's true motives and intentions in this case remain obscure, the strength of the joint force would have been sufficient to engage and defeat any advancing forces. Provided Iraqi leaders understood this danger of proceeding, and the objective of the mobilization had not already been satisfied, it can reasonably be inferred that deterrence prevailed.

Force Structure Implications of MTWs

To identify force mixes appropriate for deterrence at the MTW level, it is instructive to look at the current U.S. deployments in Korea and Southwest Asia. MTW threats are few, and the two most threatening scenarios are currently being addressed effectively through military, diplomatic, and economic means. This triad of coercive strategies is essential to any long-term effort, and, because the issues involved in MTW scenarios are immense, it is generally difficult to determine when a crisis will end, suggesting that planners should hedge against the possibility of a long-term commitment. For that reason, deterrent strategies at the MTW level must incorporate sustainable mili-

---

[26]Neil Livingston, "Iraq's Intentional Omission," *Sea Power*, Vol. 34, No. 6 (June 1991), pp. 29–30.

tary forces with the ability to protect and retaliate against a well-armed adversary in a high-threat environment. This mission calls for both the permanence of ground troops and the range and striking power of air assets.

Ground troops are essential for several reasons. First, because the objective of most aggressors at this level is territorial, the deployment of ground forces, whether American or allied, directly addresses the need to take, hold, and control terrain. Second, these missions usually require lengthy deployments, and the Army has the ability both to sustain itself and to contribute to the support of other services. Finally, the presence of ground troops, though often seen as a burden on local communities, reflects and should reinforce the unity between governments and their shared commitment to a cause. This restricts an adversary's ability to believe that he can aggressively pursue his goals without provoking a response from the United States. The two MTWs studied in this section both began with an aggressor misunderstanding American intentions. Deployed ground troops clarify matters considerably.

In compellence operations, the importance of deploying robust joint forces is magnified. While ground troops should never operate alone at the MTW level, the study suggests that an even greater role should be played by air and naval forces when the mission objective centers on compelling rather than deterring an adversary. Except for operations against landlocked adversaries, the Navy provides unique compellent value as a blockading force, diplomatically and economically isolating the adversary in order to pressure him to concede to stated demands. When the application of force is necessary to compel an adversary, air assets prove particularly useful. Air power provides the ability to strike quickly and discriminately against major targets while remaining highly protected from opposing fire and the option of being safely based in Allied or CONUS facilities, further reducing the force-protection demands of an operation.[27] Furthermore, in these delicate missions, air power benefits from being amenable to

---

[27]A recent report studies the evolving threats to expeditionary Air Force basing and the demands of defending vulnerable installations through such advancements as Theater Missile Defense. See John Stillion and David T. Orletsky, *Airbase Vulnerability to Conventional Cruise-Missile and Ballistic-Missile Attacks: Technology, Scenarios, and U.S. Air Force Responses* (Santa Monica, Calif.: RAND, MR-1028-AF, 1999).

centralized control and therefore responsive to real-time crisis management at the highest levels.   That said, to sustain and protect deployed air forces, it is often necessary that they be accompanied by a robust ground presence.

One of the key factors used by an aggressor contemplating an attack is the balance of power in the immediate theater, disregarding the more abstract, and therefore contestable, elements of military power that could potentially be brought to bear by his opponent's allies.[28] The United States has identified two scenarios that threaten MTW and taken steps to address this tendency in these cases. This has emphasized two different methods, each of which offers significant deterrent value: prepositioning and forward deployment.

In Southwest Asia the United States has prepositioned military equipment and munitions to shorten the response time to deal with threatening behavior by Iraq. The ability to respond was demonstrated in Operations Vigilant Warrior (1994), Vigilant Sentinel (1995) and Desert Thunder (1997–1998). The Army maintains the AWR-5 Set (one armor brigade) ashore in Kuwait, the AWR-3 (one armor brigade, four maneuver battalions and a direct support artillery battalion) afloat in the Persian Gulf, and another armor brigade with a full division headquarters prepositioned in Qatar. The brigade in Kuwait is constantly exercised by approximately 5,000 soldiers, while the equipment afloat and in Qatar is exercised and available for troops from the United States to fall in on whenever the situation demands. The Army's position is complemented by the presence of approximately 170 aircraft, in addition to the aircraft dedicated to Operations Northern and Southern Watch. The combined presence, JTF-SWA, has successfully responded to increased tension in the theater five times since the end of Desert Storm by dramatically altering the immediate balance of power. Furthermore, JTF-SWA demonstrated its worth not only in deterring attacks on Kuwait but also in pressuring Iraq's regime during negotiations with the UN, thereby acting as a compellent force.

The second method to alter the immediate balance of power in extended deterrence is through forward deployment, the linchpin of

---

[28]Paul K. Huth, *Extended Deterrence and the Prevention of War*, p. 4.

conventional deterrence in Europe and Korea during the Cold War. This requires much greater political will than some other coercive strategies, not only on the part of the United States but also in the host country. The coercive value of strong forward deployment is unmatchable, however, and, when conflict at the MTW level is at stake, forward deployment is a prudent measure if it is possible.

STRIKES AND RAIDS

Case Analyses

Two other mission categories fall outside the spectrum of operations in that their desired effects are not directly related to the level of effort expended to achieve them. These operations, known as strikes and raids, are germane to the discussion of coercion because they represent alternatives to coercive strategies. Rather than applying pressure to valued assets or regime stability, strikes and raids address the primary objective of the mission directly through the application of pure force. Often this option follows a failed effort to compel an adversary. The two operation types relate differently to coercion and will be dealt with here in separate sections.

Strikes. A strike is an extreme, unconditional military response to a political problem, usually one caused by a failed diplomatic strategy. The decision to execute a strike suggests a total abandonment of coercion, for it deprives your adversary of any control over the situation, even the opportunity to accommodate to your demands peacefully. The occurrence of strikes is noteworthy because they pit determined adversaries with vastly disparate military capabilities against each other. Furthermore, strikes demonstrate the unique capability of the military to achieve strategic objectives against weak adversaries unconditionally and in a short amount of time.

The strikes addressed in this study are Operation Urgent Fury (the invasion of Grenada), Operation Just Cause (the invasion of Panama), Israel's strike on the Osirak reactor site, and the Soviet Union's interventions in Hungary and Czechoslovakia. Each represents a "pure force" military approach to address perceived threats to national interests. The choice to use military force to mount a strike is typically a product of the strategic requirement that the interest be secured quickly and without negotiations that could result in delay, compromise solutions, or political obstruction. The ultimate success of a strike operation should never be in doubt due to the great disparity in capability between the adversaries. The case analysis identified three key elements of strike operations that maximized their effectiveness. These characteristics were the use of overwhelming force; the speed of the entire process, including both political decisionmaking and military responsiveness; and the element of surprise.

These characteristics were present in each of the strike cases except for Operation Just Cause. This operation, whose objective was the arrest and extradition of Panamanian dictator Manuel Noriega, developed under unique circumstances that caused planners to deviate from the standard strike. Instead of attacking without warning and forgoing diplomatic efforts to achieve the aim, the planners of Just Cause issued demands and warnings suggestive of a compellence strategy. Perhaps because a major joint command, SOUTHCOM, was located in Panama, planners felt they could compel Noriega by issuing threats and slowly building up forces. If this is true, they significantly underestimated Noriega's will to resist. Because of Noriega's relative isolation and the unlikelihood of an international outcry following his apprehension, there was little risk to the United States in following a less aggressive path. In general, however, the faster a strike operation is executed the more successful it is likely to be. Just as every aggressor wishes to present the world with a fait accompli, so to should strike planners design operations that will achieve their mission before third parties can come to the aid of their adversary.

Force Structure Implications of Strikes. The forces appropriate for a strike operation depend on the nature of the target. To deny Iraq the ability to develop nuclear weapons, Israel executed a successful aerial strike while minimizing collateral damage by striking before the facility became operational. In the other four cases, where the mission objective was to effect a regime change, planners deployed rapid-reaction land forces followed by heavier troops. The value of rapid deployment was most clearly demonstrated during the Soviet intervention in Czechoslovakia to "help the Czechoslovak working people in their struggle against reactionary forces and to protect

Czechoslovakia's security against the intrigues of imperialism."[29] Airborne troops were used to seize the airport and television station during the opening stages of this operation while ground forces attacked across the borders. Because strike operations often provoke charges of illegality or hegemony, experience suggests that whichever forces can act most quickly and with a minimum of collateral damage should be chosen to initiate the attack. In this way the initiator can secure his threatened interests without interference at crucial stages of the operation and marginalize ensuing diplomatic and humanitarian complaints.

Raids. Raids involve the "swift penetration of hostile territory to secure information, confuse the enemy, or destroy installations."[30] Generally, raids have been employed to punish adversaries when more-extensive military operations have not been desirable, but the other instruments of national power have not achieved the desired outcomes. Thus they may contribute to a larger coercive strategy but are not maintained until the enemy complies with a set of demands.

This study evaluated two raids: Operation El Dorado Canyon against Libya in 1986 and the 1998 U.S. cruise missile attacks on Sudan and Afghanistan. Both operations were provoked by terrorist acts. The dimensions of the offending acts demanded a response from the United States to support its antiterrorism platform and deter future acts, but it is unclear whether either of these goals were achieved. There is a risk after every raid that it will be perceived as an act of illegal and arbitrary retaliation. For that reason, it is vital that planners identify, and verify, legitimate strategic targets, the destruction of which will directly impair the ability of the adversary to pursue aggressive policies.

Force Structure Implications of Raids. Air assets, particularly cruise missiles and other standoff munitions, or in some cases long-range artillery, are typically used to execute raids. Because the objective is

---

[29]"Message from the CPSU CC Politburo to Members of the CPSU CC and Other Top Party Officials Regarding the Decision to Intervene in Czechoslovakia, August 19, 1968," at "Prague Spring Index of Historical Documents," available at http://library. thinkquest.org/C001155/documents/, accessed April 30, 2001.

[30]Joint Chiefs of Staff, *Joint Publication 3-07*, p. III-15. Furthermore, when forces are inserted in enemy territory during a raid, they are withdrawn upon completion of the mission.

generally limited to "sending a message" by inflicting pain, there is usually little reason to incur the risks involved in creating a presence on the ground. Nevertheless, situations may exist where the operational objectives require ground forces, which will typically be special operations forces.[31] The amount and types of force employed on a raid depend on the degree of punishment desired and can be further constrained by force-protection concerns, such as using cruise missiles instead of manned aircraft to conduct the raid.

---

[31]The first publicized U.S. ground operation in Afghanistan in October 2001, a raid by Rangers against a target near Kandahar, is an example of such a case.

Chapter Four

IMPLICATIONS AND INSIGHTS

This final chapter of the report seeks to synthesize the theories and historical cases presented in the preceding chapters. We also provide an overview of ongoing U.S. coercive efforts that have a substantial military component and offer a set of general insights derived from the study.[1]

COMBINING THEORY AND CASE RESULTS

By combining the theoretical body of knowledge with the cases described above, one can glean insights about the degree of effort that might be required to coerce a future adversary and the force mix that has historically been required at different points along the spectrum of operations. Table 4.1 correlates the measure of effectiveness categories (presented in Table 2.1: Assessment Matrix—Adversary Will and Capabilities) with the case study results.[2]

Table 4.1 shows the importance of accurately assessing an adversary's will and capabilities to the prospects for successful coercion. It

---

[1]We do not discuss operations that are part of Operation Enduring Freedom, as they were still unfolding as this report went to press. Moreover, the U.S. military operations against al Qaeda, the Taliban regime in Afghanistan, and other terrorist groups in the wake of the September 11, 2001, terrorist attacks are not coercive in nature. Instead they are intended to physically defeat and eliminate adversaries that are presumed to be uncoerceable.

[2]The Appendix to this report explains how the entries in Table 4.1 were derived and provides a synopsis of each case.

Table 4.1

Case Study Analysis Compared with Adversary Will and Capabilities Matrix

Category	Case	Coercion Assessment	Result	Force Mix
A4	Vietnam (China/MTW)	Success—China deters invasion of North Vietnam	United States places constraints on operations in and over North Vietnam to avoid confrontation with China	Chinese military capabilities
B1	KFOR (Kosovo/SASO)	Success—large-scale violence in Kosovo deterred	Ongoing peacekeeping operation	Ground forces
B1	Operation Provide Relief/UNOSOM I (Somalia/SASO)	Failure—humanitarian assistance mission imperiled by deteriorating security environment	Transition to Operation Restore Hope with a mission to provide relief and restore order in southern Somalia	Ground forces; modest air and naval support (logistics)
B1	Restore Hope/UNITAF (Somalia/SASO)	Success—disruption of humanitarian assistance deterred	Met mission of facilitating humanitarian assistance	Ground forces; modest air and naval support (logistics)
B2	SFOR (Bosnia/SASO)	Success—deterred resumption of violence	Ongoing peacekeeping operation	Ground forces
B4	MFO Sinai (Sinai/SSC)	Success—confidence-building measure that deters war	Ongoing observer mission	Ground forces
C1	IFOR (Bosnia/SASO)	Success—deterred resumption of violence	Transition to SFOR	Ground forces and air support, if needed
C2	UNPROFOR (Bosnia/SASO)	Failure—force did not deter violence	Withdrawn; IFOR eventually replaces	Ground forces; modest air strikes

Table 4.1—continued

Category	Case	Coercion Assessment	Result	Force Mix
C3	Kuwait (British Intervention/SSC)	Success—Iraq deterred	Short-term deployment of British forces believed to have deterred Iraqi invasion	Joint force; ground, air, and naval presence
C3	Iraq (current/MTW)	Success—Iraq deterred	Continued presence, demonstration of commitment; ongoing operations (Northern Watch, Southern Watch)	Joint force; ground prepositioned forces and modest presence; air and naval presence
C4	Korea (current/MTW)	Success—North Korea deterred	Continued presence and demonstration of commitment	Joint force; ground, air, and naval presence (in theater)
D1	Uphold Democracy (Haiti/Strike)	Success—President Cedras stepped down in the face of invasion	Transition to peacekeeping operations in place of invasion and combat operations	Joint force; ground-centric with air and naval forces in supporting role
D2	Algeria (French Quadrillage and Morice Line/SSC)	Temporary success—flow of insurgents stopped	French change policy, flow of insurgents resumes	Ground forces
D3	Falkland Islands (Argentine Invasion/SSC)	Failure—Argentina invades Falkland Islands	British forces retake Falkland Islands; subsequently maintain increased garrison to deter future invasion	Token ground forces, subsequent joint invasion force included ground, air, and naval (provided majority of transport and air support) forces

Table 4.1—continued

Category	Case	Coercion Assessment	Result	Force Mix
D3	Allied Force (Serbia and Kosovo/SSC)	Success—Serbia acceded to NATO demands	Transition to KFOR	Air forces (USAF/USN/other NATO); ground forces not engaged
D4	Korean War (China/MTW)	Failure—UN forces occupy North Korea	China intervenes in Korean war; North Korea restored and war extended	Chinese ground and air forces
D4	Desert Shield (Iraq/MTW)	Failure—Iraq does not withdraw from Kuwait	Desert Storm ejects Iraq from Kuwait, but Baghdad not occupied	Joint and coalition forces; air, ground, and naval
E1	Urgent Fury (Grenada/Strike)	No significant coercive efforts made by U.S. before strike	Strike operation removes regime and conducts NEO[a]	Joint force; ground-centric with air and naval forces in supporting role
E1	Just Cause (Panama/Strike)	Failure—Noriega did not step down as a result of prestrike pressure	Strike operation removes Noriega from power	Joint force; ground-centric with air and naval forces in supporting role
E1	Continue Hope/UNOSOM II (Somalia/SASO)	Failure—mission creep and casualties unhinge mission	U.S. eventually withdraws from Somalia	Ground forces; modest air and naval support, which increases to provide force protection until eventual withdrawal
E2	Soviet Union Intervention in Afghanistan/SSC	Failure—Soviet Union forces in Afghanistan do not deter mujahideen resistance	Soviet forces withdraw	Joint force; ground-centric with air in major supporting role (strike and logistics)

Table 4.1—continued

Category	Case	Coercion Assessment	Result	Force Mix
E2	El Dorado Canyon (Libya/Raid)	Ambiguous outcome	Libya punished for state sponsorship of terrorism by raid—deterrent effect still debated	Air forces (USAF and USN)
E2	Russian Intervention in Chechnya/SSC	Success—Russia crushes revolt and stops separation of Chechnya, deterring possible repeats elsewhere	Continued Russian presence and counterinsurgency operations	Joint force; ground-centric with air in supporting role (strike)
E4	Korean War (Korea/ MTW)	Failure—North Korea invades South Korea	North Korea not deterred from invading South Korea; UN forces defeat North Korean forces in the field, drawing China into the conflict	Combined UN force; ground, air, and naval
E4	Osirak Reactor (Iraq/Strike)	N/A	Iraqi nuclear program delayed	Air forces
E3	Vietnam War (U.S. versus North Vietnam/SSC)	Failure—U.S. does not deter North Vietnamese materiel support of the war in South Vietnam, neither does it compel the North to cease operations in the South	U.S. withdraws from Vietnam	Combined force; ground war in the South with air and naval support; air war in the North (USAF/USN)
E?	Infinite Reach (Sudan/ Afghanistan/Raid)	Failure—U.S. does not deter al Qaeda terrorist attacks	Raid has negligible affect on al Qaeda activities	USN cruise missiles

[a]NEO = noncombat evacuation operations.

also shows that operations at the lower end of the spectrum (SASO and low-level SSCs and strikes) are generally conducted by force mixes dominated by ground forces. High-end SSCs and MTWs generally require a mixed joint force. The size of the force of course depends on the capabilities of the potential adversary. Raids, given their inherently punitive nature, are generally executed by air or naval forces or special operations forces. Finally, in cases where coercion did not succeed—or the intervention that followed the coercive effort failed—an underestimation of the will of the adversary tends to be fundamental to the failure.

MAJOR ONGOING U.S. MILITARY COERCION EFFORTS

Although U.S. foreign policy includes a host of elements intended to help deter a vast number of states and nonstate actors from committing a wide variety of acts, a relatively small number of coercive efforts dominate the U.S. security agenda. There are two regions in which U.S. forces are maintained on relatively high levels of alert to deter MTWs: Korea, where U.S. forces have been deployed since 1950, and Southwest Asia, where U.S. troops have been deployed in the Persian Gulf region since the beginning of Operation Desert Shield in 1990. In addition to these areas, the military capabilities of the United States are postured to contribute to the deterrence or resolution of less major, or less likely, conflicts around the world. Some of these involve deployments of forces to deal with specific contingencies, ranging from peace enforcement in Kosovo to providing advice and assistance to counterinsurgency efforts in Colombia.

Another important aspect of U.S. deterrence efforts is the more general capabilities that the United States maintains to intervene in relatively unanticipated conflicts, through such means as the forward presence of naval forces and the ability to airlift light Army forces and deploy air power to areas of instability on short notice. Because much of the deterrent purpose of these capabilities lies not in resolving crises but in preventing them from even occurring in the first place, the effects of such investments are difficult to assess with any precision. However, the objective of contributing to global stability by maintaining the ability to intervene even in conflicts not foreseen far in advance is nevertheless a central element of U.S. security policy.

MTW Deterrence—Korea

Since the end of the Korean War in 1953, the United States has maintained military capabilities in South Korea with the goal of deterring attack by North Korea, or defending the South if deterrence fails. The size of these forces, particularly of their ground component, has declined in recent years as South Korea's military capabilities have increased. Today, the United States maintains a force of fewer than 36,000 troops in South Korea, the majority belonging to the Eighth Army, which fields two armor brigades and the 2nd Infantry Division, comprising a total of some 27,000 troops. In addition to the Air Force Element stationed on the Yongsan Army Post in South Korea, the U.S. forces include Air Force fighter wings based in Japan and Okinawa and a variety of naval vessels, including one aircraft carrier battle group and one Marine amphibious ready group, in the western Pacific. In the event of a North Korean attack, these would be reinforced by CONUS-based air, sea, and land forces, including Army heavy brigades, whose personnel would be airlifted to Korea, where they would man prepositioned equipment sets. These prepositioned sets diminish the need for rapid deployment because "they focus on the initial 15 to 30 days of the campaign while the United States' strategic sustainment base gears up."[3]

U.S. forces in Korea contribute to deterrence on several levels. First, they contribute to South Korea's ability to defeat an invasion, thus making a successful North Korean conquest very unlikely.[4] Army forces play a much smaller role in this deterrence by denial than does U.S. air power, however, because South Korea already possesses large and capable ground forces, and it is likely that in the event of an invasion the deployment of additional air power to the theater would be the combatant commander's highest reinforcement priority, along with the easily transported Army personnel to man prepositioned equipment. Second, the presence of U.S. forces in Korea makes it essentially impossible for Pyongyang to launch an invasion of the South without embarking on a major war with the United

---

[3]Thomas A. Schwartz, "Statement of General Thomas A. Schwartz, Commander in Chief, United Nations Command/Combined Forces Command and Commander, U.S. Forces Korea, Before the Senate Armed Service Committee: March 27, 2001" (Washington, D.C.: Senate Armed Service Committee, 2001).

[4]See O'Hanlon, "Stopping a North Korean Invasion."

States, a deterrent effect largely independent of U.S. ability to deploy additional forces to the theater, either rapidly or slowly. Finally, the defense of South Korea also poses a threat of punishment against the North, for the fight would be exceptionally bloody for the invaders, and a successful defense of the South might well lead to a UN counteroffensive to occupy the North. However, it appears likely that North Korea's interests in reunifying the peninsula under its control are extremely high, so that if achieving this objective appeared possible, it would be willing to pay a very high price to do so.

MTW Deterrence—Iraq

The other principal U.S. coercive effort is far more complex. In Southwest Asia, the United States and its allies maintain a substantial military force devoted to deterring Iraq from attacking its neighbors and from using its air force to attack internal enemies in the Kurdish north or the Shiite south.[5] Additional objectives of this effort include supporting the economic punishment of Iraq through implementing UN trade sanctions, and compelling Iraq not to attack U.S. and British aircraft operating in its airspace.[6] During much of the 1990s, the West also sought to compel Iraq to cooperate with the UN weapons inspection regime established after the Gulf War, although at the time of writing this no longer appears to be a central focus of U.S. policy toward Iraq.

The U.S. forces engaged in this effort as of early 2001 include more than 10,000 soldiers deployed throughout the region, including an armor brigade and divisional headquarters stationed in Qatar,

---

[5]These forces would also be available if necessary to defend the Gulf states against potential attack or intimidation from Iran and thus also contribute to the deterrence of such a threat.

[6]The compellent goal of the economic sanctions is somewhat ambiguous. Although they are often presented as a coercive instrument to force Iraq to comply with the terms under which the Gulf War was ended in 1991, statements by officials of the Clinton administration indicated that the United States would lift the sanctions only when Saddam Hussein was removed from office, so they are probably best seen as a brute-force policy of economic warfare intended to achieve the direct result of weakening and destabilizing Iraq, rather than as a coercive policy intended to change Baghdad's behavior (John Mueller and Karl Mueller, "The Methodology of Mass Destruction: Assessing Threats in the New World Order," *Journal of Strategic Studies*, Vol. 23, No. 1 [March 2000], pp. 163–187).

approximately 170 warplanes based in Saudi Arabia and Kuwait, and the headquarters of the Fifth Fleet in Bahrain. In the event of a major confrontation with Iraq, these troops could be quickly reinforced by Army units falling in on prepositioned equipment. One armor brigade equipment set is positioned ashore in Kuwait and materiel for another heavy brigade, supported by four maneuver battalions and a direct support artillery battalion, is positioned afloat in the Persian Gulf. Beyond ground reinforcements during a crisis, a large number of aircraft could deploy from Europe and the United States to well-equipped bases in Turkey, Saudi Arabia, and the smaller Gulf states. As in the case of Korea, developing the ability to rapidly deploy additional medium-weight forces to the theater in relatively small numbers would have little effect on the deterrence situation in the Gulf because of the substantial forces already deployed or prepositioned in or near the region.

In concert with the forces of U.S. allies in the region, and in light of Iraq's military weakness following the Gulf War and a decade of economic sanctions, this military capability is sufficient to present Iraq with a powerful threat of denial should Saddam Hussein contemplate aggressive action abroad. As in Korea, the presence of U.S. forces in Kuwait presents Iraq with the near certainty that another attack against that country could not occur without drawing the United States into the war. This is reinforced by a credible punitive threat that if Iraq invaded Kuwait or any of its neighbors, it would elicit a coalition military response that would eventually culminate in occupation of Iraq and Saddam's removal from office. U.S. efforts to deter attacks against aircraft patrolling the no-fly zones have met with less success, perhaps in part because the costs inflicted by retaliatory attacks against Iraqi air defense targets have not been great.[7]

Ongoing Non-MTW Coercive Operations Involving U.S. Military Forces

In addition to deterrent efforts in Korea and Southwest Asia, U.S. armed forces are deployed for coercive purposes in a number of

---

[7]For a detailed discussion of U.S. coercive successes and failures against Iraq since 1991, see Daniel L. Byman and Matthew C. Waxman, *Confronting Iraq: U.S. Policy and the Use of Force Since the Gulf War* (Santa Monica, Calif.: RAND, MR-1146-OSD, 2000).

smaller operations around the world. Many of these involve very limited numbers of troops in low-profile operations, but some represent quite substantial commitments of personnel and equipment.

In Kosovo, NATO's KFOR peace enforcement force includes some 50,000 troops from some 37 countries, first deployed to the province in June 1999 following the Operation Allied Force air campaign. The U.S. component of KFOR, Task Force Falcon, includes approximately 7,000 Army troops, supported if needed by NATO air power. KFOR's coercive role includes both deterring unauthorized Serbian incursions into Kosovo and compelling the Kosovars to abide by the agreements that ended the war for Kosovo. Nearby in Bosnia, the 6,600 U.S. Army troops of Task Force Eagle serve as part of NATO's 20,000-strong SFOR peacekeeping force, charged with deterring Bosnian Serbs, Croats, and Muslims from violating the 1995 Dayton peace agreement and compelling them to implement the provisions of Dayton that have not yet been embraced. As in Bosnia, the U.S. Air Force's 16th Air Expeditionary Wing at Aviano Air Base, Italy, provides a large part of the NATO air power available to support the peacekeepers, should it be required.

U.S. forces play a very different coercive role as part of MFO Sinai, where approximately 1,000 American troops constitute just under half of the multinational force tasked with monitoring the Egyptian-Israeli border following the return of the Sinai peninsula to Egypt under the Camp David accords. MFO Sinai contributes to deterrence of a future Israeli-Egyptian war primarily by minimizing each side's fears of the status quo, thus reducing the incentives for aggression. However, the MFO's interposition between Egyptian and Israeli forces would also increase the political costs to either U.S. ally of launching an attack upon the other, thus adding a punitive component to their ensuring deterrence role. The deterrent value gained as an interposed force is undermined by the force structure of the MFO. The soldiers do not have the mobility or the troop strength necessary to canvas the entire region. As a result, a determined aggressor could conceivably invade the Sinai without encountering soldiers from the MFO. Fortunately, the likelihood of this happening is greatly reduced by the transparency provided by the MFO.

In the SASO range of the spectrum, U.S. forces are deployed to a variety of actual and potential trouble spots. About 500 military advisors from the U.S. Army and other armed services provide counsel and training to Colombian government forces engaged in coercive counterinsurgency and counterdrug operations against the FARC (Revolutionary Armed Forces of Colombia) and other rebel groups. The operation, known as Plan Colombia, appears to have many flaws. Plan Colombia identifies a coercive goal, deterring farmers and drug dealers alike from participating in the production of cocaine, as the primary aim. To this end, Plan Colombia trains and equips Colombian military units. The Colombian military, while also concerned with the cocaine industry, has several other pressing missions, including countering two revolutionary groups. Having already supported the government, the United States has abandoned any chance of impartiality. At the same time, a congressionally mandated force cap prevents more robust commitment, suggesting that no conclusive end-state can be reached. Finally, the parties involved have no ability to communicate effectively with each other. The targeted drug producers have no incentive to stop producing drugs so long as Plan Colombia continues to inflict only modest punishment, the profits to be won by continuing in the drug trade outweigh those risks, and no attractive alternative to the drug trade exists or is conveyed. These difficulties are compounded by the availability of refuge both in Venezuela and in territory controlled by FARC rebels. These factors suggest that Plan Colombia will not prove effective in its present form and mission statement.[8]

INSIGHTS FOR THE FUTURE

The process whereby the military component of a coercive regime is planned is described in *Joint Publication 5-0: Doctrine for Planning Joint Operations*. At the highest levels, the Chairman of the Joint Chiefs of Staff guides the preparation of a national military strategy that addresses broad military options supportive of the national security strategy, with the advice of the Joint Chiefs and the operational commanders. Additionally, net assessments are conducted to determine the capabilities of potential adversaries as com-

---

[8]For further detail, see Angel Rabasa and Peter Chalk, *Colombian Labyrinth* (Santa Monica, Calif.: RAND, MR-1339, 2001).

pared with the United States and its potential partners.[9] Thus, "the joint operation planning process entails the development of the best possible plans for potential crises across the range of military operations involving forces that can reasonably be expected in a CINC's area of responsibility."[10]

Flexible deterrent options (FDOs) are developed to deter or defeat aggression and other challenges to U.S. interests.[11] The Army has defined FDOs as "a range of options short of engaging in combat . . . that are activities that send a clear signal to a potential aggressor of the Untied States' intent to defend a threatened vital interest."[12] Furthermore, in current Army doctrine, "A key characteristic of [FDOs] is that they do not put U.S. forces at risk until the political decision has been made to apply decisive military force. In a no-warning scenario, when the decision has been made to deploy U.S. forces, the CINC's response should call for projecting sufficient force to win

---

[9]Joint Chiefs of Staff, *Joint Publication 5-0: Doctrine for Planning Joint Operations* (Washington, D.C., 1995), I-5.

[10]Ibid., cover letter by the Chairman of the Joint Chiefs of Staff.

[11]Joint Chiefs of Staff, *Joint Publications 1: Joint Warfare of the Armed Forces of the United States* (Washington, D.C., 2000), IV-5. This publication provides the following description of FDOs: "**Use of Flexible Deterrent Options.** To deter or defeat aggression and other challenges to its interests, the United States must be able to employ variable combinations of the instruments of national power. Therefore, the United States maintains capabilities and plans to exercise tailored mixes of diplomatic, economic, informational, and military instruments to reinforce deterrence and cope with the outbreak of conflict. These flexible deterrent options call for detailed peacetime planning by the combatant command and supporting agencies involved. Many of these options are under control of nonmilitary agencies. Senior military leaders are responsible for providing advice and recommendations on the military aspects of flexible deterrent options to the NCA. Combatant commanders are responsible for preparing and employing trained, ready, and exercised force elements when the options are put into action."

[12]Ibid., IV-4-5. See also Joint Chiefs of Staff, *Joint Publication 1-02: Department of Defense Dictionary of Military and Associated Terms* (Washington, D.C., 2001), p. 163, where FDO is defined as: "A planning construct intended to facilitate early decision by laying out a wide range of interrelated response paths that begin with deterrent-oriented options carefully tailored to send the right signal. The [FDO] is the means by which the various deterrent options available to a commander (such as economic, diplomatic, political, and military measures) are implemented into the planning process."

quickly, decisively, and with minimal friendly casualties."[13] Our
sense from this study is that the Army's definition is perhaps too
limited to cover all situations. We strongly believe that a role also
exists for rapidly arriving ground forces, supported by robust joint
and/or coalition capabilities, whose sufficiency is measured in their
coercive potential rather than solely in their decisive war-winning
capability.

Several insights have emerged from this study that should be of use
in the future as the United States develops coercive strategies. First,
the assessment of an adversary is fundamental to the process of
developing a coercion strategy. This includes a net assessment not
only of an adversary's capabilities but also of the adversary's will. In
the cases we examined where coercion (or intervention) failed, the
failure can generally be traced to a misreading of an adversary's will.
Furthermore, the intelligence needed for an assessment of the
adversary's will generally lies outside military channels and will
require coordinated interagency efforts to realize. Second, when
crafting joint force packages for a coercion strategy, ground, air, and
naval forces have certain capabilities and liabilities that should be
taken into consideration. Table 4.2 attempts to capture the relative
positive attributes and potential liabilities of the U.S. armed services.

With regard specifically to the use of ground forces in coercion
strategies or interventions, several insights have emerged:

- At the lower end of the spectrum of operations, early arriving and
  capable ground forces often have high value. Indeed, in SASO
  (where population control is essential—e.g., KFOR in Kosovo)
  and strikes (where the objective is to change a regime that has
  marginal capabilities—e.g., Operation Just Cause), ground forces
  offer the most, and often the only, effective military option.

- At the higher end of the spectrum (where U.S. ground forces are
  not already present), early arriving ground forces demonstrate
  U.S. commitment, to both friends and foes, and they potentially
  deny the aggressor the prospect of an easy victory—but with

[13]U.S. Army, *FM 100-17: Mobilization, Deployment, Redeployment, Demobilization*
(Washington, D.C., 1992), p. 2, available at http://www.adtdl.army.mil/cgi-bin/atdl.
dll/fm/100-17/10017ch1.htm, accessed May 5, 2001.

Table 4.2

Positive Attributes and Liabilities of the U.S. Armed Services

Service	Ground Forces	
	Positive Attributes	Potential Liabilities
Army	Clear commitment by "boots on the ground" because of liabilities	Requires sufficient mass relative to the adversary (correlation of forces), particularly before conducting offensive operations
	Can remove a regime	Not easily removed once deployed
	Can compel enemy forces to respond to maneuver	Large sustainment dimension
	Can fix enemy forces, thereby increasing vulnerability to fires	Large force-protection dimension (potential for casualties)—requires high political will
	Ability to take, hold, and control terrain/territorial objectives	Slower to deploy robust combat capability (but pre-positioned equipment helps)
	Can be deployed in harm's way preemptively	More provocative to local populace by its very presence
	Intense, concentrated firepower	Potential target for terrorists
	Ability to control or interact directly with local populace	
	Forced-entry capability	
Marines	Similar characteristics to the Army, but also including the following:	Similar characteristics to the Army, but also including the following:
	Continuous presence with Navy without going ashore	Not sustainable in the long term ashore without Army logistics
	Highly developed NEO capability	Limited range of action and mass
		Slow deployment unless already in theater
		Limited initial capabilities

Table 4.2—continued

Air and Naval Forces

Service	Positive Attributes	Potential Liabilities
Air Force	Can deploy rapidly Ability to range over entire theater Ability to strike quickly Significant effects against important targets Ability to use force discriminately against many (but not all) targets Ability to strike deep inside enemy territory Ability to tie down enemy forces Ability to significantly restrict, if not preclude, maneuver Low risk of significant casualties	Less of a clear demonstration of commitment than ground forces (particularly if not deployed in the theater in harm's way) In certain situations (complex terrain, against irregular forces) relatively ineffective against deployed troops Expeditionary air power may requires in-theater bases; overflight permission may be an issue SAM and sensor improvements may increase air power's vulnerability in the future Possibility of collateral damage
Navy	Similar characteristics (air components) to the Air Force, but also including the following: Continuous presence, and can be deployed preemptively without bases Recognized U.S. signal Significant effects against important targets with unmanned systems (cruise missiles, naval gunfire, etc.)	Similar characteristics to the Air Force, but also including the following: Not as clear a demonstration of commitment as ground forces (but more than Air Forces not deployed to the theater) Adversary must be within range of seaborne forces Limited ability to apply sustained force (compared with land-based forces) Potentially vulnerable to future asymmetric threats Slow to deploy (other than assets in theater)

some risk. Unless ground forces are operating in an environment of air superiority and with substantial joint presence to compensate for the lack of mass of the initial ground force vis-à-vis the adversary, they can be at risk (e.g., Task Force Smith during the Korean War). Therefore, some form of joint or coalition support must be available in theater in situations where the adversary has significant capabilities in order to enable the buildup of friendly ground forces. In short, ground trip wires must have substantial joint capability behind them if they are to be militarily as well as politically significant.[14]

- Modest in-place U.S. ground forces (e.g., Korea, Southwest Asia, Bosnia, Kosovo), backed up by joint and coalition capabilities, have a significant deterrent value and provide a regional stabilizing effect. They also deny the adversary the prospect of an easy victory and send a clear signal of U.S. commitment. Finally, they provide a base around which follow-on U.S. forces can form.

- Historical examples that might support the hypothesis that an early arriving ground force can preclude aggression by an adversary are ambiguous, although the threat of an imminent airborne assault did result in Raul Cedras's leaving power in Haiti in 1994. This is particularly so in the case of an adversary who has significant capabilities. Again, what early arriving ground forces primarily demonstrate is U.S. resolve: They are the harbinger of a much larger, overwhelming follow-on force (e.g., Operation

---

[14]See Davis, "Improving Deterrence in the Post-Cold War Era," in *New Challenges for Defense Planning*, p. 219. Davis advocates developing ground forces that support the Army Transformation vision of a more lethal, deployable, and survivable force that "could be put in harm's way early, so as to demonstrate commitment and protect politically important boundaries or locations. They could also provide a formidable defensive challenge and hope to do so while surviving." Davis also notes the importance of backing up these early arriving ground forces: "it is the height of folly to establish tripwires without having the will and capability to respond massively to attacks on such a force. Tripwires can be, and often have been, tripped. The nation has moral obligations to any of its military personnel that it places in jeopardy." Even in the case of Desert Shield, the early arriving 82nd Airborne Division, which began deploying to Saudi Arabia on August 8, 1990, was rapidly backed up by other Army and joint forces, as well as by coalition forces, both already in theater and en route. By September 1, U.S. forces in Saudi Arabia totaled 95,965 personnel, of which 31,337 were Army (Frank N. Schubert and Theresa L. Kraus, eds., *The Whirlwind War: The United States Army in Operations Desert Shield and Desert Storm* [Washington, D.C.: U.S. Army Center of Military History, 1995], pp. 52, 157).

Desert Shield), and thus their specific military capabilities are less important than their political significance.

- Unsuccessful interventions (e.g., Vietnam, Somalia) can have lasting effects beyond the realm of military operations in that they can negatively affect U.S. political will, reduce the credibility of U.S. military deterrence abroad, and raise potential adversaries' perceptions of the contestability of U.S. power.

- Deterrence and intervention successes that do not remove the preconditions that caused the conflict can lead to long-term commitments to ongoing coercive regimes (e.g., Korea, Southwest Asia).

As the United States develops national security and national military strategies for the future security environment, the challenges become complex. Although the more familiar threat of cross-border, interstate aggression is still a possibility that must be deterred in some regions, new and different threats will have to be addressed in the future. Internal wars, which have external dimensions because of their threat to U.S. interests, their humanitarian dimensions, and their effect on U.S. public opinion, may again require action. Furthermore, the nature of future threats, particularly with the proliferation of WMD and international terrorism, will require new approaches to deterrence, both in the realm of homeland security and the protection of U.S. citizens and interests abroad. This report, however, shows that several aspects of devising a coercive strategy have not changed. One must understand not only an adversary's capabilities and the threshold that must be reached to coerce him but must also effectively communicate to him that you have both the will and the capability to prevail.

CASE STUDIES

The case study summaries that follow are included in this study to provide historical context to the main body of the report and to further illuminate the categorizations that appear in Table 4.1 (Case Study Analysis Compared with Adversary Will and Capabilities Matrix). They also provide additional information about the cases for readers not familiar with them. Although the case synopses are by no means comprehensive historical accounts, each case includes a footnote listing sources where more-extensive information can be found.

SUPPORT TO CIVIL AUTHORITIES (SCA) [1]

Case: Los Angeles Riots (Los Angeles, California, 1992) [2]

Category. B1. The rioters in Los Angeles had no military capability, although they did have the capacity for violence and mayhem. It appears that the presence of uniformed, armed military personnel was a significant element in deterring the rioters, thus reducing the level of violence and looting.

---

[1]As discussed above, these three cases were not included in the analysis in Chapter Three but are described here to complete the picture of how military forces may be used for coercion across the spectrum of operations.

[2]William H. Webster, *The City in Crisis* (Los Angeles: Office of the Special Advisor to the Board of Police Commissioners, 1992); William W. Mendel, "Combat in Cities: The LA Riots and Operation Rio," available at http://call.army.mil/call/fmso/fmsopubs/issues/rio.html, accessed November 15, 2000.

Result. Within a week of the deployment of uniformed military personnel, the level of violence in Los Angeles receded to a level that it could again be dealt with by civilian law enforcement agencies.

Case Synopsis. The 1992 Los Angeles riots provided three unique opportunities to study coercive strategy at the SCA level. The beginning of the riots coincided with the announcement of the not guilty verdict in the highly public trial of officers in the Los Angeles Police Department (LAPD) charged in the videotaped beating of Rodney King. At 4:15 p.m. on April 29, 1992, slightly more than an hour after the verdict was announced, crowds began looting in South Central Los Angeles. The riot escalated overnight and peaked on the second day, with elevated levels of lawlessness continuing until May 4. By the time order was fully restored, 54 people had died, 2,383 had been injured, and about $717 million of property damage had occurred.

The response to the riot followed three distinct phases. The first phase consisted of the failure of the LAPD to deter and contain the rioting in the opening day of the crisis. The LAPD's response to this highly predictable event was hampered by an "emergency 'plan' so general and unspecific, untested, unfamiliar to those who were later called upon to carry it out, and largely nonresponsive to the nature of the civil disturbance that occurred, that it proved to be essentially useless."[3] On the evening of April 29, elements of the California National Guard (CANG) were called up, marking the second phase of the riot response. The first element of the CANG to deploy, the 3rd Battalion, 160th Infantry (Mechanized), 40th Division, required almost a full day to become operational in the city. Frustrated by the slow deployment, civil authorities requested federal assistance and the CANG was federalized on May 1, marking the third phase.

The federal response, which materialized on May 3, was designated Joint Task Force–Los Angeles (JTF-LA). The Army contributed 2,023 soldiers from the 7th Infantry Division, and the Marine Corps contributed 1,508 troops from Camp Pendleton. These forces, along with the 10,465 National Guardsmen under federal control, operated in Los Angeles County until May 8 and were completely withdrawn by May 10. During their stay, the violence subsided markedly. JTF-

---

[3]Webster, *The City in Crisis*, p. 16.

LA was assisted by other agencies, including the FBI (1,200 agents), Bureau of Alcohol, Tobacco, and Firearms, Bureau of Prisons, U.S. Customs Service, and Immigration and Naturalization Service.

Case: Operation Rio (Rio de Janeiro, Brazil, 1994–1995)[4]

Category. B1. The criminal element in Rio de Janeiro had no military capability, although it did have large number of arms and had demonstrated the capacity for violence and lawlessness. The presence and operations of uniformed, armed military forces deterred further large-scale criminal activity.

Result. Operation Rio resulted in a rapid decline in criminal activity, capture of large numbers of weapons, and the reestablishment of a condition in Rio de Janeiro in which the rule of law could again be enforced by civilian law enforcement agencies.

Case Synopsis. Operation Rio was a federal effort to reestablish the rule of law in Rio de Janeiro during the early summer (November to January) of 1994–1995. During the early 1990s, the exploding population of the city, combined with an absence of government services and police protection, led to a steep increase in organized crime. The government had no effective control over large areas of the city, which became the scene of shootings, gang activity, bank robberies, and rampant drug trafficking. The state and local governments authorized the use of federal troops to restore and maintain order.

The Brazilian operation focused first on isolating the targeted areas by establishing a cordon around them. This barrier was intensively patrolled by police to restrict the movement of the criminals and interrupt contact between them and outside sources of money and arms. Finally, for three months, the task force conducted raids against specific targets inside the isolated area. The mission statement restricted both the length of the operation and the authority of federal troops, who were in effect defederalized and required to arrest suspects and participate in their eventual prosecution. Martial law was never declared and the operation was conducted under

---

[4]William W. Mendel, "Operation Rio: Taking Back the Streets," *Military Review,* Vol. 77, No. 3 (May–June 1997), pp. 11–17.

heavy media attention. Because of the rapid decrease in criminal activity throughout the city, the large number of weapons recovered, and the absence of unintended deaths or injuries, Operation Rio was officially and publicly considered a success.[5]

To achieve this success, the Brazilian government dedicated substantial military assets to Operation Rio. The core of the Task Force was formed by four Army infantry battalions and one battalion of Army military police. Further ground forces included two Marine battalions and two State Police SWAT battalions. A squadron of Army helicopters provided logistics and communications support during combat missions, and a squadron of Air Force search and rescue aircraft also participated. Force protection was complemented by a battalion of Air Force military police and civil and federal police. Finally, Operation Rio was supported by joint and interagency intelligence assets and a joint Special Operating Task Force.

Case: Desegregation of Central High School (Little Rock, Arkansas, 1957–1958)[6]

Category. B1. The element protesting the integration of Central High School did not have a military capability but posed a real threat to the nine black students attempting to attend the school. The presence of armed soldiers deterred violence against the students.

Result. The presence of armed soldiers deterred violence against the black students. Integration of Central High School was accomplished without extreme violence.

Case Synopsis. In accordance with the landmark 1954 Supreme Court ruling in *Brown v. Board of Education*, Arkansas began a well-structured process of desegregating its public education system. In 1957, following the orderly and successful desegregation of several state universities, the Little Rock school board voted unanimously to begin desegregating local high schools. Arkansas Governor Orval

---

[5]Ibid.

[6]Robert W. Coakley, Paul J. Scheips, and Vincent H. Demma, *Use of Troops in Civil Disturbances Since World War II, 1945–1965* (Washington, D.C.: Office of Military History, U.S. Army, 1971), and Robert W. Coakley, *Operation Arkansas* (Washington, D.C.: Histories Division, Office of the Chief of Military History, Department of the Army, 1967).

Faubus opposed these plans and, against the wishes of both the mayor and school board, called up the Arkansas National Guard to physically bar the admittance of the nine black students who were to begin classes on September 3. Although the public protests predicted by Governor Faubus failed to materialize, the National Guard did succeed in preventing the desegregation of Central High School.

On September 20, a court ruled against Governor Faubus and the National Guard was withdrawn. The nine black students again attempted to attend Central High School, succeeded in entering the school, but could not stay because of the danger posed by approximately 1,000 protesters. On September 24, the mayor of Little Rock appealed to President Dwight Eisenhower for assistance, requesting first U.S. Marshals, then federal troops. Eisenhower agreed to send soldiers, and that evening 1,200 soldiers from the 101st Airborne Division began arriving in Little Rock. The president also federalized the Arkansas National Guard, thereby nullifying the governor's ability to directly frustrate federal law. The next day the soldiers from the 101st escorted the nine black students into Central High School.

The soldiers of the 101st created an imposing presence. On September 25, soldiers drove the students to the school in a convoy of machine-gun armed jeeps with a helicopter escort. Each student was accompanied throughout the day by an armed soldier. The soldiers of the 101st were redeployed in November, but the Arkansas National Guard stayed at the school until the end of the academic year.

STABILITY AND SUPPORT OPERATIONS (SASO)

Case: UNPROFOR/IFOR/SFOR (Bosnia, 1992–present)[7]

Subcase A: UNPROFOR in Bosnia, 1992–1995

Category. C2. The Bosnian Serbs had modest but significant military capabilities, and while they were inclined to expand their terri-

---

[7]Christopher Bennett, *Yugoslavia's Bloody Collapse* (New York: NYU Press, 1995); Laura Silber and Allan Little, *Yugoslavia: Death of a Nation* (New York: TV Books/Penguin USA, 1996); Karl Mueller, "The Demise of Yugoslavia and the Destruction of Bosnia: Strategic Causes, Effects, and Responses," in Robert C. Owen, ed., *Operation Deliberate Force: A Case Study in Air Campaigning* (Maxwell AFB, Ala.: Air University Press, 1999), pp. 1–36.

torial control, they were deterrable when confronted by substantial military force.

Result. UNPROFOR did not ultimately deter further attacks by the Bosnian Serbs, including the seizure of Srebrenica. The conflict was finally halted by NATO air strikes and a Bosnian-Croat offensive in late 1995.

Subcases B and C: IFOR and SFOR in Bosnia, 1995–present

Category. C1 (IFOR), B2 (SFOR). Following Operation Deliberate Force and the Dayton Accords, the Bosnian combatants, primarily the Serbs, had limited military capabilities and little motivation to resume fighting in the face of NATO peacekeeping forces.

Result. Resumption of the Bosnian war has been deterred since 1995, although compelling the parties to carry out their other commitments under the Dayton Accords has been only partially successful to date.

Case Synopsis. In response to fighting between Croat and Serb forces supported by the Yugoslavian Republic from which Croatia split in 1991, the Secretary General of the United Nations appointed Cyrus Vance as his Special Envoy for Yugoslavia. Vance succeeded in negotiating a cease-fire and reaching a consensus among the Yugoslav parties that an international peacekeeping force should be deployed to the region. On February 21, 1992, the UN Security Council approved the creation of the UN Protection Force (UNPRO-FOR) to conduct peacekeeping operations in the former Yugoslavian republics. The initial mission of UNPROFOR focused on the defense and disarmament of the population in Serb-held Croatian enclaves designated as UN Protected Areas. In June 1992, the focus began to shift toward peace enforcement in Bosnia and Herzegovina, ultimately leading to an expanded mandate calling for the establishment of safe areas, the partial disarmament of the population, delivery of humanitarian aid, and patrolling and enforcing no-fly zones.

UNPROFOR originally consisted of only 50 special military observers deployed to Croatia. This number eventually grew to 38,599 military peacekeepers supported by 803 civilian police and more than 2,000

international civilian staff, the majority of whom were deployed in
Bosnia and Herzegovina.[8] The United States contributed airlift
assets to aid in force deployment and the distribution of humanitarian aid and in Operation Deny Flight deployed an aircraft carrier and
made available land-based air assets to assist in the enforcement of
the no-fly zone and provide ground attack capabilities as required.
The United States also contributed 300 ground troops to support
UNPROFOR operations in Macedonia and an additional 448 ground
troops throughout the theater.

The international peacekeeping force deployed to Bosnia and Herzegovina was flawed from the outset. In a report on the greatest failure
of UNPROFOR, the Bosnian Serb Army's massacre of ethnic Muslims
at Srebrenica in June 1995, the UN admits that the force deployed
was inadequate to the needs of the crisis and accepts blame for trying "to create—or imagine—an environment in which the tenets of
peacekeeping—agreement between the parties, deployment by consent, and impartiality—could be upheld."[9] Upon the expansion of
the UNPROFOR mandate to include enforcement of safe areas and
disarmament in Bosnia and Herzegovina, the force commander "had
estimated an additional troop requirement of approximately 34,000
to obtain deterrence through strength, [while] the Secretary-General
[Boutros Boutros-Ghali] stated that it was possible to start implementing the resolution under a 'light option,' with a minimal troop
reinforcement of around 7,600. That option represented an initial
approach and had limited objectives. It assumed the consent and
cooperation of the parties and provided a basic level of deterrence."[10] Although troop concentration in the area of operations
steadily increased through 1995, UNPROFOR was never able to deter
the threat posed by the Bosnian Serb Army or achieve its primary
mission of disarmament and protecting the population. As a result of
these failures, and following NATO's Operation Deliberate Force
bombing campaign and a successful ground offensive by Croatian

---

[8]On the origins of UNPROFOR, see Lewis MacKenzie, *Peacekeeper: The Road to Sarajevo* (Vancouver: Douglas and McIntyre, 1993).

[9]Kofi Annan, "Report of the Secretary-General Pursuant to General Assembly Resolution 53/35," p. 108.

[10]United Nations Department of Public Information, "United Nations Protection
Force," September 1996, available at http://www.un.org/Depts/dpko/dpko/co_
mission/unprof_b.htm, accessed May 22, 2001.

and Bosnian government forces in autumn 1995, a new peace set-
tlement was negotiated and UNPROFOR disbanded to be succeeded
by three distinct UN operations and a new international military
presence led by NATO.

On December 14, 1995, the Dayton Peace Accords were signed,
establishing the conditions under which a new peacekeeping mission might begin in Bosnia and Herzegovina. Six days later, NATO
troops began Operation Joint Endeavor and deployed the Implemen-
tation Force (IFOR) to Bosnia and Herzegovina. The original IFOR
consisted of 60,000 soldiers and had a one-year mandate to bring
about and maintain the end of hostilities, separate belligerent factions within the region, and collect and store heavy weapons. These
missions were accomplished by June 1996 and allowed for the withdrawal of 28,000 soldiers by December of that year. At that point,
IFOR was redesignated the Stabilization Force (SFOR) and charged
with the maintenance and enforcement of stable conditions and
coordinating with civilian organizations to support their efforts. The
remaining force of 32,000 peacekeepers from some 30 nations
remained in place until the security situation improved, and then it
was further reduced to 20,000 soldiers.[11]

The United States contributed 20,000 troops to the original deployment of IFOR. This force, primarily Army soldiers, was complemented by an Air Expeditionary Force (AEF) based in Aviano, Italy,
from which missions to enforce the no-fly zone were conducted. The
AEF also provided the capability of conducting air strikes, though
this action never proved necessary. The United States maintained
this strength until June 1998, when its presence was reduced to 6,800
soldiers. This number was gradually reduced thereafter, most
recently in May 2001, leaving the U.S. presence in Bosnia at 3,200
soldiers, out of a total of 28,000 peacekeepers. The coalition force
performs regular patrols throughout their area of operations and
continues to coordinate with civilian organizations operating in
Bosnia and Herzegovina.

---

[11]NATO, "NATO Fact Sheet: NATO's Role in Bosnia and Herzegovina," August 2000,
available at http://www.nato.int/docu/facts/2000/role-bih.htm, accessed May 22,
2001.

Case: Operations Provide Relief (UNOSOM II), Restore Hope (UNITAF), and Continue Hope (UNOSOM II) (Somalia, 1992– 1994)[12]

Subcase A: Operation Provide Relief (UNOSOM I: August 15– December 9, 1992)

Category. B1. Somali factions were armed with light weapons, rocket-propelled grenades, and machine guns. Although they did not meet the criterion of having a "modest capability" in terms of being an organized military threat, the factions did have the capacity for significant violence, especially inside Mogadishu.

Result. The forces deployed in UNOSOM I, although they did initially enable a significant humanitarian assistance effort, were not able to deter the eventual disruption of relief supplies by Somali warlords. In the face of this disruption, the UN operation was reinforced and became UNITAF.

Subcase B: Operation Restore Hope (UNITAF: December 9, 1992– May 4, 1993)

Category. B1. Same as Subcase A, above.

Result. UNITAF was largely successful in its dual mission of providing humanitarian assistance and restoring order in southern Somalia.

Subcase C: Operation Continue Hope (UNOSOM II: May 4, 1993– March 31, 1994)

Category. E1. Although still possessing the capabilities mentioned in Subcases A and B above, Somali factions, particularly those of Somali warlord Mohammed Farah Aideed, resisted UN attempts to restore order and actively engaged UN forces in combat.

---

[12]John L. Hirsch and Robert B. Oakley, *Somalia and Operation Restore Hope: Reflections on Peacemaking and Peacekeeping* (Washington, D.C.: United States Institute of Peace Press, 1995); Mark Bowden, *Black Hawk Down: A Story of Modern War* (New York: Atlantic Monthly Press, 1999); Lawrence E. Casper, *Falcon Brigade: Combat and Command in Somalia and Haiti* (Boulder, Colo.: Lynne Rienner, 2001); James O. Tubbs, *Beyond Gunboat Diplomacy: Forceful Applications of Airpower in Peace Enforcement Operations* (Maxwell AFB, Ala.: Air University Press, 1997).

Result. UNOSOM II was a peace enforcement mission whose goals included disarming the Somali clans and establishing a secure environment throughout Somalia. Eventually, this mission resulted in an escalation of the level violence, which could no longer be deterred, followed by the withdrawal of U.S. and UN forces.

Case Synopsis. In 1992, the UN responded to a devastating famine and the disintegration of government control in Somalia by implementing Operation Provide Relief. The operation was designed to deliver humanitarian aid to the Somali population by deploying a limited number of observers supported by UN peacekeepers designated as UNOSOM. The scope of the problem, particularly the observers' inability to control the distribution of aid, quickly overwhelmed the effort. Confident that greater stability in Somalia could facilitate the distribution of aid and avert a humanitarian disaster, the United States proposed and won UN endorsement of a second mission to Somalia called Operation Restore Hope, or UNITAF (for "unified task force").

UNITAF was built around the U.S. 1st Marine Expeditionary Force. In total, the United States contributed 28,000 personnel, including 10,300 U.S. Army soldiers, and other nations contributed close to 10,000 troops. The forces participating in UNITAF included soldiers from Australia, Belgium, Botswana, Canada, Egypt, France, Germany, Greece, India, Italy, Kuwait, Morocco, New Zealand, Nigeria, Norway, Pakistan, Saudi Arabia, Sweden, Tunisia, Turkey, the United Arab Emirates, the United Kingdom, and Zimbabwe. The entry force of U.S. Marines landed unopposed in the Somali capital, Mogadishu, on December 9, 1992, secured the airfield at Baledogle on December 13, and on December 16 occupied the southern town of Baidoa, which was the key staging area for relief missions in the interior of the country. These early successes were followed by operations to improve the local infrastructure, confiscate heavy crew-served weapons, and escort convoys, all in order to speed and ensure the distribution of humanitarian aid. Casualties were rare and UNITAF naturally ingratiated itself to the population. As mandated by the original charter, preparations were made to transfer authority to a UN peacekeeping force designated UNOSOM II in order to provide for the withdrawal of military forces.

The third and final stage of U.S. operation in Somalia began on May 4, 1993. The immediate crisis of famine having passed, the mission in Somalia turned to the restoration of law and order in hopes that a functioning civil society might protect the welfare of the population. The majority of U.S. soldiers were withdrawn, leaving only 28,000 peacekeepers to enforce an expanded mandate that included the general disarmament of the population. The remaining U.S. soldiers consisted of 4,500 soldiers, which included a 1,150-man Quick Reaction Force provided by the 10th Mountain Division (Light). The more expansive mission of UNOSOM II clashed with the authority of local warlords, and UN forces became, in effect, co-belligerents. In June, a detachment of Pakistani peacekeepers was ambushed with the loss of 24 men by the forces of Mohammed Farah Aideed, a prominent Somali warlord.

In response to the ambush of the Pakistanis, the UN passed Security Council Resolution (UNSCR) 837, which called for the immediate apprehension of those responsible. This led to a hunt for Aideed by a detachment of U.S. Special Operations forces deployed in late August under the name Task Force Ranger. The more aggressive strategy pursued by UNOSOM II, and the level of force applied to achieve the expanding number of goals, eventually frayed the relationship between the force and the population they were sent to assist. The degree to which this relationship had deteriorated became clear on October 3, 1993, when Task Force Ranger soldiers and helicopter crews came under heavy fire by an enraged mob of Somalis. That day, 18 American soldiers were killed and 78 wounded. The effect this event had on the mission, particularly the U.S. role, was palpable. Rather than continue to escalate the level of violence in Mogadishu, U.S. commanders retreated into fortified bases, rarely dispatching soldiers to conduct reconnaissance for the remainder of the operation. U.S. troops were withdrawn from Somalia in March 1994.[13]

---

[13] Allard, *Somalia Operations,* pp. 13–20. See also Bowden, *Black Hawk Down.*

SMALLER-SCALE CONTINGENCIES (SSCs)

Case: Multinational Force and Observers (MFO) Sinai (Sinai Peninsula, 1982–present)[14]

Category. B4. Both Israel and Egypt have substantial military capabilities; the MFO Sinai has very modest military means.

Result. The MFO Sinai has, by its presence, contributed to the deterrence of renewed conflict between Israel and Egypt.

Case Synopsis. Under the terms of the 1979 Camp David Peace Accords, the Sinai peninsula was returned to Egypt after 12 years of Israeli occupation following the Six-Day War. Israel agreed to withdraw to its pre-1967 border and the Sinai would become a demilitarized and "restricted force" zone. Although a force of UN observers had existed on the Sinai since 1948, it had withdrawn during times of hostility and demonstrated no ability to preserve peace or deter conflict in the region. The arrangement agreed to in 1979 and implemented fully in 1982 called for a U.S.-organized detachment of soldiers and observers to supervise the treaty and promote transparency and trust between Egypt and Israel.

Today, 11 countries participate in the MFO, fielding a force of some 1,900 troops. The United States is by far the largest contributor of forces, deploying 895 soldiers, along with troops from Colombia, Fiji, Italy, Uruguay, Hungary, Canada, Australia, New Zealand, France, and Norway. Although the force is centered around observers and logistics support, there are small detachments of fixed-wing aircraft, helicopters, and maritime support. Having operated for close to two decades, deploying troops to the Sinai has become routine. In a recent announcement, Secretary of Defense Donald Rumsfeld suggested that the United States might withdraw from the MFO. This suggestion drew protests from both Egypt and Israel who credited the MFO with providing a key source of stability in a troubled region.[15]

---

[14]For information on the mission and history of the MFO Sinai, see http://www.mfo.org.

[15]Jane Perlez, "Rumsfeld Seeks to Withdraw American Troops from Sinai," *New York Times,* April 19, 2001, p. A1.

Case: British Intervention in Kuwait (1961)[16]

Category. C3. Iraq had built up substantial military capabilities and appeared to be prepared to annex Kuwait in the absence of substantial defensive forces.

Result. Deterrence appears to have succeeded following the rapid deployment of British forces to Kuwait, as Iraq withdrew the forces it had been massing on the border.

Case Synopsis. A week after Kuwait became a fully independent state in 1961, having been a British protectorate since 1899, Iraqi President Abdul Karim Kassem announced his intention to annex the newly proclaimed country, over which Iraq had a long-standing territorial claim, and Iraqi forces began moving south from Baghdad. Within two days of this announcement the Kuwaiti emir, Abdallah al-Salim Al Sabah, requested British military assistance. The British response was immediate and apparently effective, providing an example of either the successful deterrence of cross-border aggression or the gross misinterpretation of Iraqi diplomatic signals. It is unclear whether Iraq seriously intended to attack, but if so this threat never materialized and the crisis ended peacefully.

The British response came in two stages: the first secured points of disembarkation inside Kuwait, the second established a line of defense along the Kuwait-Iraq border. The operation was most notably characterized by the speed of its execution. Deployment was greatly accelerated by the fact that the 42 Royal Marine Commando was onboard HMS *Bulwark* off Karachi at the time of the crisis. These troops immediately headed to Kuwait where they secured landing areas and the airport by the morning of July 1, two days after Kuwait requested assistance. These initial entry forces were supported by 45 Commando, stationed in Aden, followed by airlifted British infantry from Bahrain and Kenya and paratroopers stationed in Cyprus and the United Kingdom. Arrival of the latter was delayed several days because Turkey refused to grant overflight rights.

---

[16]Phillip Darby, *British Defence Policy East of Suez, 1947–1968* (London: Oxford University Press, 1973), pp. 244–249; Peter Mangold, "Britain and the Defence of Kuwait, 1956–71," *RUSI Journal*, September 1975, pp. 44–48; Mustafa M. Alani, *Operation Vantage: British Military Intervention in Kuwait, 1961* (Surbiton, UK: LAAM, 1990).

Almost immediately after arriving in Kuwait and securing the points of entry, British soldiers established a line of defense along the border. Although light troops alone would have been overwhelmed by an Iraqi attack, the British soldiers were supported by two squadrons of RAF fighters quickly deployed to Kuwait from Aden and Kenya, arriving on July 1, bombers and other aircraft deployed to Bahrain and Sharjah, and soon by the aircraft carrier HMS *Victorious*, which was dispatched from the South China Sea at the outset of the crisis. By October, Arab League members had generated a force sufficient to take over the mission, their strategic aim being not so much to deter Iraq as to replace the British. The British were able to withdraw completely by October 19. Their experience in Kuwait highlights both the inherent ambiguity of successful deterrence and the advantage of global engagement and forward deployment.

Case: Argentine Invasion of the Falkland Islands (1982)[17]

Category. D3. Argentina possessed substantial military capabilities relative to those of the UK, and had a high coercion threshold.

Result. Britain failed to deter the invasion of the Falklands, underestimating both the Argentine regime's strong motivation to invade the islands and Argentina's willingness to discount the UK's capability and will to liberate them.

Case Synopsis. In 1982, the long-standing dispute between the United Kingdom and Argentina over possession of the Falkland Islands, known as the Islas Malvinas in Argentina, escalated into a major military conflict that resulted in the loss of close to 1,000 British and Argentine personnel and several warships. This study focused primarily on the opening stages of the Falklands War in order to describe and critique the British strategy for deterring an Argentine attack.

---

[17]Anthony H. Cordesman and Abraham R. Wagner, *Lessons of Modern War, Volume 3: The Afghan and Falklands Conflicts* (Boulder, Colo.: Westview, 1991); Max Hastings and Simon Jenkins, *The Battle for the Falklands* (New York: W.W. Norton and Company, 1984); The *Sunday Times* of London Insight Team, *War in the Falklands: The Full Story* (New York: Harper & Row, 1982).

Prior to the crisis, the Argentine government was facing intense internal pressure. Street demonstrations throughout 1981 had weakened the military junta that had taken power in a 1976 coup, and in December 1981 a new junta assumed power. This government felt pressure to produce an early victory to increase its popularity and enhance the prestige of the military.[18] Indications that the United Kingdom was decommissioning its only naval vessel stationed in the region contributed to the impression that an invasion of the Falkland Islands would be an easy affair, unopposed by the British, as well as essential to the regime's survival.[19]

At the time of the invasion, March 2, 1982, only 67 British Marines were on the Falklands. Even this token force was actually twice its normal strength because the invasion came during the garrison's annual rotation cycle. Despite increasing tensions, including an uprising by Argentine workers on neighboring South Georgia Island, which lies about 900 miles to the east, and a history of contention with Argentina over the sovereignty of the island groups, no attempt was made by the British to reinforce the garrison or deter an attack on the Falklands in the weeks leading up to the invasion. Even in the two days preceding the invasion, after British intelligence sources had warned that an attack was imminent, no extraordinary measures were taken by the military to support a coercive policy that might avoid war. Argentina pressed ahead with the invasion and occupied the islands until they were reconquered by British forces in June 1982.

The Falklands conflict demonstrates several elements of coercion, including the importance of clearly communicating commitments, deploying adequate forces for the protection of contested territory, and understanding what stresses on one's adversary might result in highly risk-acceptant behavior, all of which the British failed to do.

---

[18]*The Sunday Times* of London Insight Team, *War in the Falklands*, pp. 60–65.

[19]*The Portsmouth News*, "Falklands: 15 Years On" (Portsmouth, UK: Portsmouth Publishing and Printing, 1997), pp. 5–15.

Case: Operation Uphold Democracy (Haiti, 1994–1996)[20]

Category. D1. Haiti had negligible military means but refused U.S. and UN coercion efforts until the threat of significant military means was employed.

Result. The threat of a U.S. military strike coerced the resignation of Raul Cedras and enabled the permissive deployment of U.S. forces into Haiti.

Case Synopsis. Following the ouster of President Jean-Bertrand Aristide in 1991, the government of Haiti fell into the hands of a series of irresponsible and malevolent military dictators, the last of whom was General Cedras. Despite early signs of cooperation with the UN, Cedras abandoned his 1993 pledge to return Aristide to power, prompting the UN to reimpose economic sanctions. The sanctions, combined with the violence perpetrated against the population by the military regime, resulted in untenable conditions for the Haitian people, many of whom fled the country by sea, seeking asylum in the United States. In response to the outrages being committed in Haiti and the humanitarian crisis resulting from the flood of refugees, the United States formed a multinational force in support of a UN-mandated military intervention. The intervention, Operation Uphold Democracy, resulted in the successful and peaceful occupation of the island nation in September 1994. The ultimate mission of stabilizing the society and restoring democratic institutions was undertaken in March 1995 by a UN-led force under the name Operation Restore Democracy.

Throughout the negotiations leading up to Operation Uphold Democracy, the United States and the UN clearly communicated to the Cedras regime their demands for Aristide's reinstatement and the dissolution of the military junta. To add weight to these demands and in support of the original 1993 agreement (the Governors Island Accords) the United States dispatched the USS *Harlan County* to the Haitian capital, Port-au-Prince. The USS *Harlan County*, a tank

---

[20]John R. Ballard, *Upholding Democracy: The United States Military Campaign in Haiti, 1994–1997* (Westport, Conn.: Praeger, 1998); Lawrence E. Casper, *Falcon Brigade*; Eloisa Green, "Haiti: Operations Other Than War," *Foreign Military Studies Office Special Study*, No. 94-93 (1997).

landing ship (LST), carried on board Joint Task Force HAG. JTF HAG consisted primarily of an Army Special Forces Company, a platoon of Marine Military Police, a Navy Construction Battalion, and a Royal Canadian Air Force Engineer detachment. The ship entered Port-au-Prince harbor on October 11, 1993, unescorted, presuming a permissive entry based on negotiated agreement. Instead, the USS *Harlan County* was opposed by an unruly armed mob on the docks and harassed in port by armed motorboats. Faced with this unexpected opposition and unequipped and lacking the mandate to force an entry into Haiti, the captain of the USS *Harlan County* remained until the afternoon of the next day, when he withdrew to Guantanamo Bay, Cuba. This early attempt to compel an end to the violence on Haiti proved unsuccessful and is believed to have damaged American credibility in future negotiations with the Cedras regime.[21]

In response to the deterioration of conditions within Haiti and the growing refugee problem posed by Haitians fleeing their country, the United States mounted Operation Uphold Democracy in September 1994. The military preparations were conducted in concert with ongoing diplomatic negotiations with the Cedras regime to avoid the necessity of a forced entry. Two task forces of light troops, one made up of soldiers from the 82nd Airborne Division, the other from the 10th Mountain Division, trained and assembled for Operation Uphold Democracy to accommodate to the need for either a peaceful or forced entry. The decision on September 17 to go ahead with a forced entry by the 82nd Airborne did not rule out the possibility of a last-minute change. Indeed, negotiations between Cedras and a special delegation of Jimmy Carter, Sam Nunn, and Colin Powell arranged for the unopposed entry of soldiers already en route to Haiti. The credibility gained by the delegation as a result of the commitment of soldiers is uncertain. However, it is clear that until Cedras was faced with the certainty of a military intervention he did not accommodate to the multinational force's demands. The majority of U.S. troops were withdrawn from Haiti in 1995. However, through the end of 2000, the U.S. Army maintained a force of approximately 200 soldiers to perform security, medical, and civil assistance missions.

---

[21] Peter J. A. Riehm, "The USS *Harlan County* Affair," *Military Review*, Vol. 77, No. 4 (July–August 1997), pp. 31–36.

Case: French Quadrillage and Morice Line (Algeria, 1957– 1958)[22]

Category. D2. The insurgents in Algeria possessed a modest military capability and their supporters were bent on infiltrating support into Algeria.

Result. The significant investment by the French in the Morice Line deterred infiltration into Algeria, but its cost proved unsustainable and the effort ultimately failed.

Case Synopsis. The Algerian Civil War stands out as one of the most vicious conflicts in modern history. Rather than study the entirety of the war, which continued in various forms from 1954 to 1974, this report focused on a single phase of the French involvement known as the Quadrillage. The French had been engaged in Algeria since 1830 and persisted in the civil war from 1954 until 1962. In 1956, France granted independence to Tunisia and Morocco, the better to focus their efforts on Algeria. Their efforts were hampered, however, by supporters of the Algerian cause in the newly independent states who infiltrated supplies and fighters across the border. To isolate the Algerian conflict, the French erected elaborate defenses along the Algerian border. This effort to compel an end to efforts to aid the Algerian FLN (Force Liberation Nationale) approached pure force yet ultimately proved to be an effective, though unsustainable, coercive strategy.

The border defenses, known as the Morice Line after the French Defense Minister, were completed in 1957. Extending 450 kilometers along the Tunisian border and 750 kilometers along the Moroccan border, the Morice line consisted of barbed wire, followed by a minefield, followed by an eight-foot-high electrical fence. About 80,000 French soldiers, out of a total force of 400,000 in Algeria, were concentrated along the line to prevent insurgents from infiltrating across the frontier and to pursue those who succeeded. The defenses achieved their purpose, cutting external support to the FLN by 90 percent, capturing 4,600 weapons, and resulting in the death of 6,000 FLN soldiers. The effort required to sustain the defenses, however,

---

[22]Brush, "The Story Behind the McNamara Line."

soon exhausted the French Army and led to an abandonment of this strategy after only seven months.

Case: Chechen Insurgency (Chechnya, 1994–present)[23]

Category. E2. The Chechen insurgents have a modest military capability and appear determined to form an independent state.

Result. Despite early setbacks, the Russians have prevented the separation of Chechnya, although an active state of guerrilla warfare persists.

Case Synopsis. Chechnya, a region in the Northern Caucasus mountain range, declared independence from Russia in 1993. This action resulted in a civil war that brought Russian troops into the province in 1994. The subsequent Russian military involvement in Chechnya is generally divided into two parts. The first, from 1994 to 1996, resulted in the deaths of several thousand Chechen citizens and several hundred Russian soldiers without resolving the question of Chechen independence or creating conditions for a stable peace. The second phase, from 1999 until the present, has so far resulted in the destruction of the Chechen capital of Grozny by Russian forces that, in turn, sustain mounting casualties from guerrilla attacks. With the exception of the temporary Russian withdrawal from 1996 to 1999, neither side has succeeded in destroying its adversary's will or ability to mount a significant resistance.[24]

Following months of clandestine involvement and support of pro-Russian Chechen factions, the Russian military intervened openly in the Chechen conflict in December 1994. Attempting to quickly establish control over Grozny, three Russian armored divisions, supported by pro-Russian Chechen forces and Russian internal security units, launched an invasion of Chechnya. Entering the city, the Russian forces found themselves vulnerable to well-organized resistance, resulting in the loss of hundreds of tanks and other armored

---

[23]See Olga Oliker, *Russia's Chechen Wars, 1994–2000: Lessons from Urban Combat* (Santa Monica, Calif.: RAND, MR-1289-A, 2001).

[24]Casualties sustained by both sides are poorly reported and vary greatly. The Chechen population suffered severely during both phases of Russian operations in the region, while the Russian forces were seriously harmed during the first.

vehicles and mounting pressure from the public to withdraw from the conflict. In 1996, a cease-fire was negotiated, leaving the question of Chechen independence to be decided at a later date.

In October 1999, the Russian military launched a more concerted campaign to establish control over the region. The attack again centered on Grozny, but during this operation extensive use of artillery and aerial bombardment leveled much of the city before Russian ground forces entered. As a result, Russian casualties were much lower during the second siege of Grozny. The Russian military also did a more effective job of controlling media access inside Chechnya, thereby avoiding much of the public outcry that accompanied the earlier campaign. Despite greater success in capturing the capital, Russian forces have struggled to gain control over Chechen rebel forces in the mountainous countryside and are frequently subject to guerrilla attacks.

Case: Operations Allied Force and Joint Guardian (Kosovo, 1999–present)[25]

Subcase A: Operation Allied Force, 1999

Category. D3. Serbia possessed substantial military capabilities, and Serb President Slobodan Milosevic was strongly motivated to resist NATO demands that Serbia cede control of a major part of its territory.

Result. Serbia complied with NATO's compellent demands to withdraw its forces from Kosovo following an 11-week bombing campaign.

Subcase B: Operation Joint Guardian, 1999–present

Category. B1. Kosovar Serb and Albanian groups possess modest ability to commit violence against each other and limited motivation to do so in the presence of NATO peacekeepers.

---

[25]Clark, *Waging Modern War;* Byman and Waxman, "Kosovo and the Great Airpower Debate"; Bruce R. Nardulli et al., *Disjointed War: Military Operations in Kosovo, 1999* (Santa Monica, Calif.: RAND, MR-1406-A, 2002).

Result. Substantial violence in Kosovo has largely been deterred since the arrival of KFOR.

Case Synopsis. The international response to the crisis in Kosovo transpired in two basic phases. The first phase, named Operation Allied Force, compelled the Serbian Army and internal security forces to withdraw from Kosovo. The second phase, named Operation Joint Guardian, deterred aggression between the Kosovo Liberation Army and the Serbian Army and paramilitary groups while protecting the population from unorganized social unrest. Both operations, at this point, can be considered successful coercion.

Kosovo, a province in southern Serbia, has a population with a large majority of ethnic Albanians. Kosovo had enjoyed a large degree of autonomy within Yugoslavia since 1973, but, when the federal state disintegrated in 1989, President Milosevic revoked Kosovo's local autonomy. The crisis began in earnest in 1998 when the Serbian Army's and security forces' campaign against Kosovar rebels resulted in the deaths of more than 1,500 Kosovar Albanians and the internal displacement of 400,000 refugees. Concerned for the welfare of the Kosovar Albanians and the fragile peace being maintained throughout the region, the UN Security Council issued a declaration on March 31 expressing its interest in the matter and determination that the violence stop. In support of this resolution, NATO identified two primary goals regarding the crisis in Kosovo:

- to help achieve a peaceful resolution of the crisis by contributing to the response of the international community; and

- to promote stability and security in neighboring countries with particular emphasis on Albania and the former Yugoslav Republic of Macedonia.[26]

This resolution allowed NATO to consider an active military role in the developing Kosovo crisis. This role proved necessary in October. On October 13, 1998, NATO approved air strikes against Serbian targets in a move to support of a diplomatic mission calling for the safe

---

[26]NATO, "NATO Fact Sheet: NATO's Role in Response to the Conflict in Kosovo," available at http://www.nato.int/kosovo/history.htm, accessed May 9, 2001.

return of refugees to their homes in Kosovo and permission to deploy a team of international observers. These conditions were agreed to.

In 1999, Kosovar and Serbian officials failed to reach agreement at talks held in Rambouillet, France. Following the breakdown in negotiations, the Serbian government moved tanks and additional forces into Kosovo, violating their earlier agreement and exacerbating the refugee crisis. Again, a diplomatic mission to Serbia was backed by the threat of NATO air strikes, though in this case Milosevic was not coerced into compliance. His defiance led directly to Operation Allied Force, which began on March 23, 1999, and lasted until June 10.

Operation Allied Force's goal was to compel the complete withdrawal of Serbian military and paramilitary forces from Kosovo in order to create conditions for the deployment of a NATO peacekeeping mission to the region. In support of this mission, NATO aircraft flew 10,484 strike sorties over the 78 days of Operation Allied Force. The United States contributed approximately 730 of some 1,055 aircraft used in Operation Allied Force. The largest contingent of planes served as part of the Air Force's 31st Air Expeditionary Force, based in Aviano, Italy, along with U.S. Marine fighter-attack and electronic warfare aircraft. The U.S. Air Force also contributed a large contingent of KC-135 tankers and flew bombing, refueling, reconnaissance, and airlift missions from air bases in Germany, England, the Middle East, and CONUS. The Navy contributed the aircraft of the USS *Theodore Roosevelt* carrier battle group and ships and submarines armed with land-attack cruise missiles, and it also kept a Marine Expeditionary Force in the theater. The Army deployed Task Force Hawk, a force based around attack helicopters, to Albania in the later stage of the conflict.

During most of Operation Allied Force, attacking aircraft generally stayed above 15,000 feet to reduce the risk of losses from Serbian air defense systems. Together with extreme reluctance to cause civilian casualties, this restriction limited the effectiveness of air strikes against certain targets, such as camouflaged tanks. Beyond targeting these smaller military assets, however, NATO attacked strategic targets inside Serbia, such as oil refineries, electrical utilities, bridges, television stations, and government offices. With its infrastructure devastated, its forces inside Kosovo increasingly vulnerable to attacks by the paramilitary Kosovo Liberation Army, and the threat of an eventual NATO invasion of Serbia looming on the long-term horizon, the Serbian leadership was compelled to withdraw its forces from the region and to permit an international peacekeeping force to enter Kosovo. The UN accepted the terms of the agreement and called for the immediate deployment of an international force to Kosovo.

On June 12, 1999, the first elements of KFOR arrived in Kosovo to undertake Operation Joint Guardian, the deterrence phase of the mission. Their entry, coordinated with the withdrawal of the Serbian Army, proceeded peacefully and was greatly speeded by the pre-deployment of soldiers to the Macedonia-Kosovo border under UNPREDEP. The first U.S. troops to arrive in Kosovo belonged to a Marine Expeditionary Force (1,700), Task Force Hawk (1,900), and approximately 200 soldiers based in Germany tasked with setting up a joint headquarters. The Marine and Task Force Hawk contingents were soon withdrawn, and a regular Army force deployed from Germany. By late 1999, approximately 7,000 soldiers formed the U.S. contribution to a total KFOR deployment of 50,000 soldiers.

The primary goal of KFOR was to facilitate the return of refugees to their homes by creating a safe environment. Accomplishing this mission required KFOR soldiers to establish a high level of presence throughout the region, de-mine roads, confiscate heavy weapons, and create a concentrated presence along the Serbia-Kosovo border. The resolution also called for the training of a professional, ethnically mixed security force to gradually replace the international presence and an investigation of war crimes to prepare for possible prosecution. Although these tasks are conducted primarily by independent agents of the UN, their work requires close cooperation with KFOR.

Case: American Intervention in Vietnam (Vietnam, 1961– 1973)[27]

Subcase A: Chinese deterrence of U.S. escalation in North Vietnam

---

[27]There is a vast literature on the Vietnam War. Two good general histories are George C. Herring, *America's Longest War*, second edition (New York: Knopf, 1986), and Guenter Lewy, *America in Vietnam* (New York: Oxford University Press, 1978).

Category. A4. The United States and China both had substantial military capability. The United States believed that China was highly motivated to prevent the escalation of the war against North Vietnam, particularly a ground invasion.

Result. China, through nonmilitary means, successfully deterred the United States from conducting a ground invasion of North Vietnam and from prosecuting a more aggressive air campaign against North Vietnam for the majority of the war (until the Linebacker bombing campaigns in 1972). The United States was deterred largely because it feared active Chinese intervention in the war, based on the precedent of the Korean War.

Subcase B: U.S. deterrence of North Vietnamese aggression in South Vietnam

Category. E3. The United States faced North Vietnam, a state with significant military power and a very high coercion threshold.

Result. The United States was unable to apply sufficient military (or nonmilitary) means to coerce the North Vietnamese into abandoning their goal of unifying North and South Vietnam. The United States viewed the conflict as a limited war. The North Vietnamese viewed it as a total war. In short, the North Vietnamese had the will to withstand the military (and other) means the United States was prepared to apply.

Case Synopsis. The American intervention in Vietnam began in December 1961 in response to the danger posed to the pro-Western South Vietnamese government by Communist guerrilla forces and the Communist government of North Vietnam. The initial deployment of 4,000 soldiers to advise and train South Vietnamese soldiers would eventually become the largest American military operation since World War II. The deployment peaked in 1969 when the American presence reached 543,000 military personnel. Despite the extensive ground, air, and naval operations in South Vietnam and air and naval operations against North Vietnam, the United States never succeeded in creating peaceful and stable conditions in the South Vietnam. The last American soldiers were withdrawn in 1973, and the South Vietnamese government fell to the attacking North in 1975.

Among the difficulties encountered by American strategists were containing Communist forces in the South and preventing supplies and main force conventional units from North Vietnam from influencing the war. The U.S. military was constrained in this regard, limiting itself to conducting ground operations only in South Vietnam, thus precluding ground intervention in North Vietnam or against the supply routes running through Laos and Cambodia. Air operations, although initially limited against the North, gradually expanded in 1964 and 1965 and even more so during heavier bombing campaigns in 1966–1968 (Operation Rolling Thunder) and 1972 (Operations Linebacker I and II).

China, a supporter of North Vietnam, opposed the American presence in South Vietnam and continually warned against U.S. offensives against North Vietnam. China also provided materiel and safe storage areas for supplies and, between 1966 and 1968, deployed soldiers to North Vietnam. Finally, China served as a deterrent against larger-scale U.S. bombing and any ground invasion of North Vietnam because the United States, chastened by its experience during the Korean War, feared a Chinese intervention in the war. The Soviet Union also provided materiel assistance, particularly in the form of sophisticated air defense systems.

Case: Soviet Intervention in Afghanistan (Afghanistan, 1979–1989)[28]

Category. E2. Afghan resistance forces possessed relatively limited military capabilities but virtually unlimited commitment to resist the Soviet occupation of Afghanistan, even at a very high price.

Result. In spite of intense efforts to compel the mujahideen to give up, which inflicted great damage and were largely unconstrained by concern with public opinion or humanitarian costs, the Soviets failed to make resistance to their occupation appear entirely hopeless or intolerably costly, and compellence failed.

---

[28]Cordesman and Wagner, *Lessons of Modern War, Volume 3: The Falklands and Afghanistan*; Edward B. Westermann, "The Limits of Soviet Airpower: The Failure of Military Coercion in Afghanistan, 1979–1989," *Journal of Conflict Studies*, Vol. 19, No. 2 (Fall 1999), pp. 39–71; Lester W. Grau, "The Soviet Experience in Afghanistan," *Military Review*, Vol. 75, No. 5 (1995), pp. 16–27.

Case Synopsis. In September 1979, Afghanistan's unpopular pro-Soviet government was overthrown in a coup led by the country's premier, Hafizullah Amin. This generated tension with the Soviet Union, which feared that a weakened central government would limit its influence in the country and might eventually pose a threat to stability in the Soviet republics on the Afghan border. In December 1979, Soviet forces began massing along the border with Afghanistan and increased their presence in the Afghan capital of Kabul to deter rebel forces from overthrowing the government and simultaneously prepare for the removal of Amin.

On December 24, 1979, Soviet special forces seized the airport at Kabul. The following day, three Soviet airborne divisions flew into the capital while four motorized infantry divisions crossed the border into Afghanistan. The Soviet forces faced resistance from both the Afghan Army and rebel forces, though within three days the forces succeeded in overthrowing Amin's government and installing a regime friendly to the Soviet Union.

Throughout 1980, rebel forces, particularly the mujahideen, increased their resistance to the Soviet occupation while international protests, including the U.S.-led boycott of the Moscow Olympic Games, condemned the Soviet action. The Soviet strategy focused on establishing defense perimeters around major cities, controlling supply routes through the mountain valleys and across the Khyber Pass to Pakistan, and launching raids and air strikes against mujahideen rebels and the villages that supported them. This strategy called for the concentration of ground troops in urban areas and the creation of air bases to supply the troops and initiate air assault operations. By 1984, 19 airports in the region had either been built or newly constructed, allowing for the extensive use of fixed-wing aircraft and helicopters. Attack helicopters proved particularly effective in the mountainous terrain and were used to prepare landing sites before the insertion of airborne soldiers. Although the Soviet government disguised from the world and its own citizens the true scope of their involvement in Afghanistan, an estimated 120,000-plus Soviet troops were engaged in Afghanistan at the conflict's height and Soviet casualties exceeded 15,000 during the course of the eight-year occupation.

The mujahideen successfully resisted Soviet forces by relying on guerrilla warfare tactics and receiving substantial amounts of military aid from Arab and Islamic countries as well as the United States. Their military capability was greatly enhanced by the delivery from 1986 of U.S.-made Stinger antiaircraft missiles. This weapon gave the mujahideen an effective defense against the airplane and helicopter attacks that had become the cornerstones of Soviet tactics. Despite being generally poorly armed and uncoordinated, and despite the devastated state of Afghanistan's economy and civilian population, the rebels showed no sign of weakening, while Soviet casualties and international and domestic pressure to withdraw from the conflict continued to escalate. In April 1988, the Soviet Union reached a cease-fire agreement and began removing its military forces, and by 1989 Soviet forces had fully withdrawn from Afghanistan. The Soviet-backed regime remained in power until 1992, when the mujahideen captured Kabul.

MAJOR THEATER WARS

Case: Gulf War and Subsequent Deterrent Operations Against Iraq (Southwest Asia, 1990–Present)[29]

Subcase A: Operations Desert Shield and Desert Storm, 1990–1991

Category. D4. Iraq possessed very large, albeit overrated, military forces and a strong incentive to resist U.S. coercive demands in the wake of the Kuwaiti invasion.

Result. Iraq was not deterred from occupying Kuwait, and even when threatened with imminent attack was not compelled to withdraw. Late in the Gulf War, Iraq pursued a negotiated withdrawal from Kuwait but complied with Allied surrender terms only after being expelled from it and when facing the threat of further military operations against Iraq.

---

[29]Cordesman and Wagner, *Lessons of Modern War, Volume 4: The Gulf War* (Boulder, Colo.: Westview, 1996); Rick Atkinson, *Crusade: The Untold Story of the Persian Gulf War* (Boston: Houghton Mifflin, 1993); Michael R. Gordon and Bernard E. Trainor, *The Generals' War* (Boston: Little, Brown, and Company, 1995); Herr, *Operation Vigilant Warrior.*

Subcase B: U.S.-led deterrence of Iraq, 1991–present

Category. C3. Iraq's military capabilities were substantially reduced by the Gulf War, and it was not inclined to launch major military operations against substantial opposition.

Result. Iraq was deterred from further attacks against Kuwait or Saudi Arabia and from major violations of the no-fly zones, in the face of U.S. and allied military forces.

Case Synopsis. The conflict between Iraq and Kuwait has evolved over the past decade and come to include several distinct elements, each of which provides material for a study of coercive strategy. This study focused on Iraq's initial aggression in 1990, the immediate American response, the coalition strategy leading up to the withdrawal of Iraqi forces from Kuwait, postcrisis enforcement of the cease-fire and no-fly zones, and ensuing efforts to address Iraqi provocations and instability throughout the region.

Iraq has laid a claim to Kuwait since the small country gained independence from Britain in 1961. In the summer of 1990, following disagreements over Iraqi debt held by Kuwait and Saudi Arabia and over oil production in a shared field, Iraq became increasingly menacing toward Kuwait. The U.S. Ambassador to Iraq, April Glaspie, met with Iraqi president Saddam Hussein on July 25 to learn Iraq's intentions toward Kuwait but did not explicitly proclaim Kuwait's territorial integrity as a vital national interest that would provoke a strong American response. Iraq moved into Kuwait on August 2, 1990, with a force of approximately 120,000 soldiers led by 2,000 tanks. At the time, Iraq had one of the largest armies in the world, estimated to stand at almost 1 million soldiers, a modern air force, and a demonstrated willingness and capability to employ chemical weapons.

The international community responded quickly. On August 5, President Bush stated unambiguously that the invasion of Kuwait would not stand and called on Iraq to withdraw immediately. The UN also condemned the action, imposed an embargo, and passed a resolution calling for the withdrawal of Iraqi troops from Kuwait. A later UN resolution, passed on November 29, authorized the use of necessary force to compel Iraq to withdraw from Kuwait.

In coordination with these diplomatic efforts, the United States and other nations began deploying military forces into the theater as a nascent coalition against Iraq. Saudi Arabia requested American military assistance on August 6. On August 7, the first U.S. forces, Air Force F-15 fighters, arrived in Saudi Arabia and the 82nd Airborne Division's second brigade began deploying. This brigade completed deployment on August 14, and by August 24 three full brigades of the 82nd were deployed to Saudi Arabia. These soldiers initially took positions alongside the Saudi Arabian National Guard. Within the first week, 4,000 U.S. Army soldiers had deployed, supported by 15 Apache helicopters, 18 Sheridan tanks, 56 TOW missile systems, two Multiple-Launch Rocket Systems, and 12 105-mm howitzers.

The Army was further supported by robust joint forces in the theater. On August 2, the day of the invasion, the Navy had two carrier battle groups in the region: one in the Mediterranean and the other in the Indian Ocean. By August 8, both of these groups were in position and capable of launching strikes against Iraqi forces. In addition, the Navy sent two Marine Expeditionary Brigades that arrived in the Persian Gulf shortly after the 82nd Airborne Division. By the end of August, more than 700 Air Force fighter and attack aircraft were in the theater. By September 1, the U.S. military presence in the Persian Gulf totaled 95,965 troops, of which 31,337 were Army.[30]

The massive buildup of forces continued for months but did not compel Iraq to abandon Kuwait. On January 17, 1991, coalition forces began conducting air strikes on Iraqi forces and other targets in Kuwait and Iraq. Coalition air attacks decimated Iraqi forces for weeks, until coalition ground forces began the attack on Iraqi forces in Kuwait and Iraq on February 24. Iraqi forces were badly beaten in every encounter and soon began surrendering and retreating en masse. A cease-fire went into effect on February 28.

The termination of Desert Storm led to the liberation of Kuwait and the creation of several missions to preserve the peace and stabilize the region. Foremost among these were Operation Provide Comfort

---

[30]U.S. Navy, Chief of Naval Operations, *The United States Navy in Desert Shield/Desert Storm* (Washington, D.C.: Naval Historical Center, 1991), available at http://www. history.navy.mil/wars/dstorm/, accessed May 24, 2001.

and Operation Southern Watch.[31] The purpose of these missions was to control Iraqi aggression against minorities inside Iraq and, in the case of Provide Comfort, to deliver humanitarian assistance to these minorities. (Operation Northern Watch succeeded Provide Comfort and focused solely on containing Iraqi aggression.) These missions were mandated by UNSCRs 678, 687, and 688 in the case of Northern Watch and UNSCRs 687, 688, and 949 in the case of Southern Watch.

To protect ethnic minorities concentrated in the north and south of Iraq, no-fly zones were established following the end of the ground offensive. Operation Southern Watch, which enforces a no-fly zone in Iraq extending south of the 33rd parallel, combines forces from United States, France, Great Britain, and Saudi Arabia. The original mandate for the operation was provided by UNSCR 688 in April 1991. Missions to enforce this resolution, prompted by Iraqi violations, began on August 27, 1992. The largest contributor to Southern Watch forces is the United States, which provides approximately 14,000 personnel for ground-based air forces and two carrier battle groups. The Air Force conducts approximately two-thirds of the sorties. Although Iraq launched fighters to confront coalition air forces during the early phase of Southern Watch, they currently resist only with antiaircraft artillery fire and missile launches. Patrolling aircraft are authorized, acting in self-defense, to target and destroy any Iraqi force posing a threat and have thus avoided suffering any losses.

Operation Northern Watch uses the same rules of engagement to patrol the no-fly zone north of the 36th parallel. Approximately 45 aircraft and 1,400 personnel are based at Incirlik Air Base, Turkey, to perform the mission. The United States contributes a joint force of approximately 1,100 soldiers to support Operation Northern Watch. Although patrolling aircraft are frequently fired on by Iraqi forces, no casualties have been suffered.

U.S. forward-deployed and prepositioned forces in the region also remain poised to confront Iraqi attacks against neighboring states. These assets were required in late September 1994, when Iraq again

---

[31]On January 1, 1997, Operation Provide Comfort ended. To continue to enforce a no-fly zone north of the 36th parallel in Iraq, Turkey, Great Britain, and the United States commenced Operation Northern Watch.

threatened Kuwait. In response to significant Iraqi armor and personnel mobilizations south of the 32nd parallel, the UN Security
Council passed UNSCR 949, condemning the movements and
demanding a demobilization. President Clinton initiated Operation
Vigilant Warrior on October 14, 1994, to demonstrate both American
resolve to contain Iraq and the military's ability to deploy quickly in
strength. Within two weeks, the United States had increased its
presence in the region from 3,500 to over 28,000 troops and deployed
more than 200 additional combat aircraft. The prepositioned afloat
AWR-3 was offloaded by elements of the 24th Infantry Division and
exercised in coordination with the prepositioned brigade in Kuwait
and the Kuwaiti National Guard. In late October, Iraq withdrew its
forces north of the 32nd parallel and American soldiers began rede-
ploying in November.

Case: The Korean War and Aftermath (Korean Peninsula, 1950–Present)[32]

Subcase A: North Korean invasion of South Korea, 1950

Category. E4. North Korea had substantial military capability and
was committed to the reunification of Korea through force.

Result. U.S. and South Korean forces were unable to deter a North
Korean invasion of South Korea. North Korea was compelled to leave
South Korea through the application of substantial military force.

Subcase B: UN invasion of North Korea, 1950

Category. D4. China possessed significant military capability and
was committed to the existence of a North Korean state.

Result. China did not deter UN forces from occupying North Korea.
China compelled the removal of UN forces when it attacked them in

---

[32]David Rees, *Korea: The Limited* War (New York: St. Martin's Press, 1964); T. R.
Fehrenbach, *This Kind of War: The Classic Korean War History* (Washington, D.C.:
Brassey's, 1998); Clay Blair, *The Forgotten War: America in Korea, 1950–1953* (New
York: Times Books, 1987); Max Hastings, *The Korean War* (New York: Touchstone,
1987). Finally, for a definitive official history, see *The United States Army in the Korean
War* series, published by the U.S. Army Center of Military History.

North Korea and drove them south of the 38th parallel. Eventually, the status quo antebellum was restored.

Subcase C: Post–Korean War divided Korea, 1953–present

Category. C4. North Korea possesses significant military capability and has positioned substantial forces along the Demilitarized Zone (DMZ) that separates the two Koreas, the assumption for some 50 years is that North Korea is committed to the forceful reunification of Korea.

Result. The United States and South Korea have maintained a significant military capability that has deterred the potential invasion of South Korea by North Korea.

Case Synopsis. The conditions resulting in the Korean War were largely established by an agreement between the United States and the Soviet Union on August 15, 1945, which determined that Soviet troops would accept the surrender of Japanese soldiers on the Korean peninsula north of the 38th parallel and U.S. soldiers would accept the surrender of Japanese soldiers south of the 38th parallel. This agreement led to the de facto division of Korea at the 38th parallel following World War II. In 1947, following an initiative by the UN, the Republic of Korea (ROK) was established in the American-held southern sector. In protest, the Soviet Union established the Democratic People's Republic of Korea (DPRK) in the north. The DPRK immediately began harassing the ROK through low-intensity conflict while cooperating with the Soviet Union to develop its armed forces. The ROK received military assistance from the United States, though in June 1949 the United States largely withdrew its soldiers from the ROK. This withdrawal was part of a realignment of U.S. priorities in Asia, which, as described by Secretary of State Dean Acheson in January 1950, included Japan, Okinawa, and the Philippines as vital American interests but not Korea.

The North Korean invasion of South Korea began on June 25, 1950. By the end of the war, three years later, 15 members of the United Nations had entered the war as a Unified Command on the side of the ROK and the DPRK had been reinforced by Communist China. The UN force suffered 118,515 killed and 264,591 wounded. Of these, 33,629 of the dead and 103,284 of the wounded were Americans. More than 10,000 Americans were captured, the majority of whom never returned. The ROK military suffered 70,000 killed, 150,000 wounded, and 80,000 captured while approximately 3 million ROK civilians died as a result of the war. The opposing Communist forces lost approximately 1.6 million soldiers. At the height of its involvement (April–July 1953), the United States deployed more than 440,000 troops to Korea: 276,581 Army, 84,124 Navy, 36,966 Marines, and 46,388 Air Force.[33]

The salient events of the Korean War, and those most pertinent to a study of coercive strategy, include the initial invasion, the initial American response, the Inchon landing, the Chinese intervention, and the armistice establishing the persistent confrontation between the DPRK and the ROK across the 38th parallel.

At the outset of the war, the North Korean Army was vastly superior to the South Korean forces. The North Korean Army was trained and equipped by the Soviet Union and consisted of approximately 130,000 men, a brigade of T-34 medium tanks, and 100,000 reserves. Some of these soldiers were veterans of the Chinese revolutionary wars in Manchuria. The North Korean Air Force was equipped with 180 World War II fighters and attack aircraft provided by the Soviet Union. South Korea, on the other hand, had no significant air force, armored force, or artillery. Its entire military power consisted of a 100,000-man constabulary force. The United States, which had avoided guaranteeing the ROK's security, possessed limited military power in the theater. The Seventh Fleet was available, and the Air Force maintained eight combat groups in the Far East Air Forces. The U.S. ground strength was limited to four divisions manned at two-thirds strength, located primarily in Japan. Artillery, tanks, and other supporting arms were in short supply.

Immediately following the North Korean invasion, the UN condemned the act, and President Truman authorized General Douglas MacArthur, commander of U.S. forces in Asia, to support the ROK with air and naval forces. On June 30, Truman extended MacArthur's mandate and authorized the use of U.S. ground troops to compel an end to hostilities. On July 5, the first element of U.S. ground intervention came into contact with the North Korean Army. Task Force

---

[33]R. Ernest Dupuy and Trevor N. Dupuy, *The Encyclopedia of Military History* (New York: Harper & Row, 1986), pp. 1, 251.

Smith, named after its commanding officer Lieutenant Colonel Charles B. Smith, consisted of 540 infantrymen lightly supported by artillery. This force positioned itself to block an advancing North Korean Division led by 30 tanks. Task Force Smith was completely overwhelmed, suffering 150 casualties and abandoning most of its equipment in a disorganized retreat. The North Korean Army advanced steadily until the ROK and its allies, by now organized as the UN Command (UNC), controlled only a small corner of the peninsula around the port of Pusan.

Following an amphibious landing at Inchon on September 15, 1950, the UNC rapidly pushed the North Korean Army out of the south, crossing the 38th parallel on October 1 and reaching the Chinese border along the Yalu River on October 28. Before the UNC crossed the 38th parallel, Chinese Premier Chou En-lai warned that China would not tolerate an invasion of North Korea. He also sent a private message to the U.S. government through an Indian official that China would intervene in the war if U.S. forces crossed the 38th parallel. As the UNC approached the Chinese border, the Communist government massed hundreds of thousands of troops along its frontier. The exact number of Chinese soldiers was unknown to MacArthur because of a prohibition on aerial reconnaissance north of the Yalu. Both MacArthur and the Central Intelligence Agency believed that Chinese forces would not attack unless China were invaded, despite Chinese statements to the contrary and evidence that Chinese forces had been operating in North Korea since early November. On November 24, 1950, MacArthur ordered an advance on the Yalu. Chinese forces attacked in strength the next day, pushing back UNC forces and eventually achieving a stalemate roughly along the 38th parallel.

Following the first year of dramatic offensives and counteroffensives were two years of punishing stalemate. An armistice signed on July 28, 1953, ended the fighting without resolving the status of Korean unification. U.S. forces remained in Korea to protect the devastated population from future Communist predations. Until the 1970s, the United States maintained a force of more than 80,000 troops in the ROK, primarily soldiers belonging to the 8th Army. Starting in 1971, this number was reduced to 43,000. The present U.S. strength of 36,000 military personnel consists of 25,000 Army, 10,000 Air Force, and detachments of Naval and Marine forces. The reduction of U.S.

presence is largely compensated for by the increasing strength of the ROK economy and armed forces that took over defense of all but one kilometer of the border in 1971.

STRIKES

Case: Operation Urgent Fury (Grenada, 1983)[34]

Category. E1. Forces opposing the U.S. strike on Grenada had negligible military capability but were committed to staying in power.

Result. Little coercive effort against the regime in Grenada before the U.S. strike. U.S. forces invaded Grenada and forced a regime change after overcoming negligible resistance.

Case Synopsis. Although the small island nation of Grenada had been run by a Socialist government since 1979, it maintained good relations with the United States until October 1983, when a military coup resulted in a more radical government and the breakdown of civil society. Worried that the increased presence of Cuban military personnel on the island signaled a pro-Communist Grenada and concerned for the safety of 800 American medical students there, the United States, in coordination with the Organization of American States (OAS), decided to take action.

President Ronald Reagan had paid particular attention to the situation on the island since a 1982 conference with Caribbean leaders in Barbados, concluding that Grenada might serve as an additional Communist beachhead in the Caribbean.[35] In March 1983, Reagan voiced his concerns regarding Grenada in an address to Congress, unambiguously identifying the threat to American national security posed by Cuban and Soviet influence in Grenada.[36] In light of these

---

[34]Ronald H. Cole, *Operation Urgent Fury: The Planning and Execution of Joint Operations in Grenada, 12 October–2 November 1983* (Washington, D.C.: Joint History Office, 1997).

[35]Julie Wolf, "The Invasion of Grenada," available at http://www.pbs.org/wgbh/amex/reagan/peopleevents/pande07.html, accessed May 20, 2001.

[36]Ronald Reagan, "Address to the Nation on Defense and National Security," March 23, 1983, available at http://www.reagan.utexas.edu/resource/speeches/1983/32383d.htm, accessed May 20, 2001.

initiatives, the October coup and the necessity of launching an invasion can be viewed as a failure in a general deterrence strategy aimed at containing Communist influence in the Western Hemisphere.

The invasion was named Operation Urgent Fury. Consisting primarily of U.S. soldiers, the force's mission was to capture the Point Salines airfield that was considered to have strategic value, to secure and evacuate the American medical students, and to replace the ruling regime with a democratically elected government. The first mission, capturing the airfield, was performed by U.S. Army Rangers, who parachuted into the target and secured it for the eventual arrival of elements of the 82nd Airborne Division. These soldiers were supported from the air by Air Force AC-130 Spectre gunships and Navy A-7 Corsairs and from sea by the USS *Caron*. The second part of the mission, securing and evacuating the American medical students, was conducted by a 400-strong Marine Amphibious Unit. The final mission, to establish a democratically elected government, was supported by U.S. Navy SEAL teams that parachuted into the theater to secure the Governor General, who was under house arrest. In all, 1,900 American troops initiated the operation, eventually climbing to a peak presence of 5,000 American and 300 OAS-member soldiers. The mission succeeded at the cost of 19 Americans dead and 119 wounded. U.S. forces were withdrawn from Grenada in 1985.

Case: Operation Just Cause (Panama, 1989–1990)[37]

Category. E1. The Panamanian Defense Forces (PDF) had a negligible military capability, but General Manuel Noriega was committed to remaining in power.

Result. Prestrike efforts to coerce Noriega into leaving office failed. U.S. forces conducted a strike that neutralized the PDF and removed Noriega from power.

Case Synopsis. General Manuel Noriega, the leader of the military regime in Panama, became increasingly hostile to American interests throughout 1989. To protect Americans and American installations

---

[37]Ronald H. Cole, *Operation Just Cause: The Planning and Execution of Joint Operations in Panama, February 1988–January 1990* (Washington, D.C.: Joint History Office, Office of the Chairman of the Joint Chiefs of Staff, 1995).

in Panama, capture General Noriega (who was accused of drug trafficking), and install a democratically elected Panamanian government, the United States executed Operation Just Cause in December 1989. Operation Just Cause was a strike designed to arrest General Noriega, who had resisted all efforts to compel him to surrender to U.S. authorities. Based on PLAN 90-2, it called for a complete neutralization and restructuring of the PDF.

To achieve this mission, the Joint Chiefs of Staff formed Joint Task Force South (JTF South). JTF South was based around a brigade of the 82nd Airborne Division, two brigades of the 7th Infantry Division, and a Joint Special Operations Task Force based on the 75th Ranger Regiment. These forces, supported by more than 145 aircraft belonging primarily to the 830th Air Division, began their attack on the PDF on December 20. The first strikes, carried out by air dropping elements of the 82nd Airborne and Ranger Regiment, were on Rio Hato, the Torrijos and Tocumen airports, and entry routes to Panama City. The support of F-117 stealth fighters and particularly AC-130 gunships was essential to the early destruction of the PDF command and control network. These entry forces were soon reinforced by the soldiers of the 7th Infantry Division. In all, JTF South required 22,000 Army soldiers, 3,400 airmen, 900 Marines, and 700 sailors. By striking quickly and employing overwhelming force against a poorly led and poorly equipped adversary, JTF South established control over the country within four days. General Noriega was eventually transferred into U.S. custody on January 3. Redeployment began that day with the ultimate target of under 10,000 soldiers, the original strength of SOUTHCOM before Operation Just Cause, being reached by the end of January. The operation officially ended January 11, 1990, with the United States having suffered 23 soldiers killed and 322 wounded, and Panama suffering 297 killed and 123 wounded.

Case: Osirak Reactor Strike (Iraq, 1981)[38]

Category. E4. Iraq was a major military power by Middle Eastern standards, and its motivation to develop nuclear weapons was extremely high.

---

[38]Victor Flintham, *Air Wars and Aircraft* (New York: Facts on File, 1990).

Result. Noncoercive strike inflicted temporary damage on the Iraqi nuclear program as intended.

Case Synopsis. The Osirak reactor facility, 12 miles southeast of Baghdad, was a centerpiece of Iraq's ambitious nuclear weapons development program. Israeli intelligence agents had long worked to impede the Iraqi nuclear program, and two unidentified F-4 aircraft, believed to be Iranian, had attacked the site unsuccessfully in September 1980, early in the Iran-Iraq War. With the plant soon expected to become operational and begin producing weapons-grade uranium and plutonium, after which bombing the reactor would release radioactive fallout, Israeli leaders ordered an air attack against the facility to be launched on Sunday, June 6, 1981. The attacking force consisted of eight F-16A fighter-bombers, each carrying two 1,000-kilogram bombs, escorted by six F-15A fighters. It crossed Jordanian and Saudi airspace prior to entering Iraq, flying at very low altitudes to avoid detection by Iraqi air defense radars and U.S. AWACS patrols over Saudi Arabia. The aircraft attacked the reactor at dusk, surprising the defenders and reportedly hitting the target with all sixteen bombs, destroying it. The Israeli aircraft then returned to base without loss after a round trip of 1,370 miles.

The Osirak attack was a highly successful aerial strike, achieving its physical objective as planned. It did not—and presumably was not intended to—deter Iraq from further efforts to develop nuclear weapons. These programs were subsequently carried on in heavily camouflaged facilities, most of which were unknown to the United States until discovered by weapons inspectors after the 1991 Gulf War, by which time they were very advanced, with Iraq's first nuclear weapons estimated to have been only several years away.

RAIDS

Case: Operation El Dorado Canyon (Libya, 1986)[39]

Category. E2. Libya had modest means relative to the U.S. military but was apparently strongly motivated to resist U.S. coercion.

---

[39]Brian L. Davis, *Qaddafi, Terrorism, and the Origins of the U.S. Attack on Libya* (New York: Praeger, 1990); David C. Martin and John Walcott, *Best Laid Plans: The Inside Story of America's War Against Terrorism* (New York: Harper & Row, 1988).

Result. The U.S. attack did not deter further Libyan-supported terrorism.

Case Synopsis. Tensions between the United States and Libya had been mounting for some years when, on April 5, 1986, a discotheque in West Berlin frequented by U.S. servicemen was bombed by terrorists. In response to evidence of Libyan involvement in the attack, the United States launched a multiservice air strike against targets in Libya, code-named Operation El Dorado Canyon, on the night of April 15–16, 1986.

Prestrike photographic and electronic reconnaissance missions were flown by U.S. Air Force and Navy aircraft from bases in Spain, Cyprus, and the United Kingdom. The central element of the attack was 18 USAF F-111F bombers, escorted by three EF-111A electronic warfare aircraft and supported by more than 60 tanker aircraft, which flew 4,000 kilometers each way from bases in England (along a circuitous overwater route through the Strait of Gibraltar because France and Spain denied overflight permission for the mission) to bomb targets in Tripoli. These included the military side of Tripoli airport, a terrorist training facility, and a military barracks that served as a command and control center and as one of Libyan dictator Col. Muammar Qaddafi's residences. Meanwhile, U.S. Navy and Marine aircraft from the *America* and *Coral Sea* carrier battle groups attacked a military airfield and a barracks near Benghazi. Damage to the targets was substantial, although significant collateral damage occurred in the area around the barracks in Tripoli, including damage to several European embassies. One F-111 was lost with its crew as the bombers flew away from their targets.

Assessing the strategic success of the raid is difficult, and 15 years later the debate continues to rage. Its inherently imprecise central objective was to deter Libyan and other support of international terrorism, and, although the overtness of Libyan support for terrorism, particularly against U.S. military personnel in Europe, did decline during the several years following the raid, Libya went on to sponsor the bombing of a Pan American 747 airliner over Lockerbie, Scotland, in 1988. Popular reactions to the attack in both the United States and Western Europe were largely favorable, although the appearance of a U.S. hard line against terrorism may have been weakened by revelations of the White House's arms-for-hostages deals with Iran during the same period.

Case: Operation Infinite Reach (Sudan and Afghanistan, 1998)[40]

Category. E?. Al Qaeda's destructive capabilities were believed at the time to be trivial by military standards, but the motivation of Osama bin Laden and his followers to resist U.S. coercion was virtually unlimited.

Result. The raids had no discernible coercive impact, and their limited nature may have encouraged the target to expect similarly mild retaliation in response to future attacks.

Case Synopsis. On August 7, 1998, two simultaneous terrorist attacks on American embassies in Kenya and Tanzania killed 224 people, including 12 Americans. Based on information that al Qaeda, a terrorist network headed by Osama bin Laden, had been responsible and was planning additional attacks in the immediate future, the United States unilaterally launched an attack on August 20 against targets inside Afghanistan and Sudan. Using Tomahawk land-attack cruise missiles launched from naval vessels, the attacks were timed to simultaneously strike four targets within Afghanistan and one target in Sudan. The targets in Afghanistan, all close to the Pakistani border, were described as training camps connected to Islamic terrorist organizations, including al Qaeda. The target in Sudan was a chemical factory in Khartoum believed to be involved in the manufacture of V-series nerve agents.

The mission of Infinite Reach was to deter future terrorist acts against the United States by demonstrating a willingness and capability to punish terrorist organizations. In addition, there was an effort to reduce future chemical terrorist threats by destroying the Sudanese factory, thereby denying terrorists access to the chemical agents it was believed to produce. Infinite Reach does not appear to have been successful. The United States continues to suspect Osama

---

[40]Mark E. Kosnik, "The Military Response to Terrorism," *Naval War College Review*, Vol. 53, No. 2 (Spring 2000).

bin Laden of promoting terrorism, including the attack on the destroyer USS *Cole* in Yemen on October 12, 2000, and the terrorist attacks in New York and Washington on September 11, 2001. The attack on the factory in Khartoum came under immediate suspicion after Sudanese officials claimed the factory was engaged in the legal manufacture of pharmaceuticals, a claim supported by Western contractors connected with the plant. Documents later revealed disagreements within the American government concerning the accuracy of the information regarding the Sudanese factory and its being included as a target in Operation Infinite Reach.[41]

---

[41]"U.S. Offensive Against Terrorism," *New York Times on the Web*, available at http://www.nytimes.com/library/world/africa/index-us-attack-terror.html, accessed May 31, 2001.

BIBLIOGRAPHY

Alani, Mustafa M., *Operation Vantage: British Military Intervention in Kuwait, 1961*, Surbiton, UK: LAAM, 1990.

Aldis, Anne, ed., *Strategic and Combat Studies Institute Occasional Paper No. 40—The Second Chechen War*, Shrivenham, UK: Conflict Studies Research Centre, 2000.

Allard, Kenneth, *Somalia Operations: Lessons Learned*, Fort McNair, D.C.: National Defense University Press, 1995.

Allison, Graham T., *Essence of Decision: Explaining the Cuban Missile Crisis*, Boston: Little, Brown and Company, 1971.

Annan, Kofi, "Report of the Secretary-General Pursuant to General Assembly Resolution 53/35: The Fall of Srebrenica," New York: United Nations, 1999.

Arquilla, John, *Dubious Battles: Aggression, Defeat, and the International System*, Washington, D.C.: Crane Russak, 1992.

_____, and Paul K. Davis, *Extended Deterrence, Compellence and the "Old World Order,"* Santa Monica, Calif.: RAND, N-3482-JS, 1992.

Atkinson, Rick, *Crusade: The Untold Story of the Persian Gulf War*, Boston: Houghton Mifflin, 1993.

Baldwin, David A., "The Power of Positive Sanctions," *World Politics*, Vol. 24, No. 1 (October 1971), pp. 19–38.

Ballard, John R., *Upholding Democracy: The United States Military Campaign in Haiti, 1994–1997*, Westport, Conn.: Praeger, 1998.

Bandow, Doug, "Leave Korea to the Koreans," available at http://www.cato.org//dailys/05-27-00.html, accessed May 2, 2001.

Baumann, Robert F., "Operation Uphold Democracy: Power Under Control," *Military Review*, Vol. 77, No. 4 (July–August 1997), pp. 13–21.

Bennett, Christopher, *Yugoslavia's Bloody Collapse*, New York: NYU Press, 1995.

Bernstein, Barton J., "Compelling Japan's Surrender Without the A-Bomb, Soviet Entry, or Invasion: Reconsidering the US Bombing Survey's Early-Surrender Conclusions," *Journal of Strategic Studies*, Vol. 18, No. 2 (June 1995), pp. 101–148.

Blair, Clay, *The Forgotten War: America in Korea, 1950–1953*, New York: Times Books, 1987.

Bonesteel, Ronald M., "Conventional Deterrence in Ethno-Nationalist Conflicts," *Military Review*, Vol. 75, No. 1 (December–February 1995), pp. 20–31.

Bowden, Mark, *Black Hawk Down: A Story of Modern War*, New York: Atlantic Monthly Press, 1999.

Brands, H. W., *The Devil We Knew: Americans and the Cold War*, Oxford, UK: Oxford University Press, 1993.

Brecher, Michael, and Wilkenfield, Jonathan, *A Study of Crisis*, Ann Arbor, Mich.: University of Michigan Press, 1997.

Brennan, Richard R., Jr., "The Concept of 'Type C' Coercive Diplomacy: US Policy Towards Nicaragua During the Reagan Administration, 1981–1988," Ph.D. dissertation, University of California, Los Angeles, 1999.

Brodie, Bernard, "Strategy as a Science," *World Politics*, Vol. 1, No. 4 (July 1949), pp. 467–488.

_____, *War and Politics*, New York: Macmillan, 1973.

Brown, Michael, *Deterrence Failures and Deterrence Strategies*, Santa Monica, Calif.: RAND, P-5842, 1977.

Brush, Peter, "The Story Behind the McNamara Line," *Vietnam,* No. 2 (February 1996), pp. 18–24.

Bush, George H. W., "Address to the Nation on the Civil Disturbances in Los Angeles, California," May 1, 1992," available at http://bushlibrary.tamu.edu/papers/1992/92050105.html, accessed May 1, 2001.

Byman, Daniel L., and Matthew C. Waxman, *Confronting Iraq: U.S. Policy and the Use of Force Since the Gulf War,* Santa Monica, Calif.: RAND, MR-1146-OSD, 2000.

_____, "Defeating U.S. Coercion," *Survival,* Vol. 41, No. 2 (Summer 1999), pp. 107–20.

_____, "Kosovo and the Great Air Power Debate," *International Security,* Vol. 24, No. 4 (Spring 2000), pp. 5–38.

_____, and Eric Larson, *Air Power as a Coercive Instrument,* Santa Monica, Calif.: RAND, MR-1061-AF, 1999.

Carter, Ashton B., and John P. White, eds., *Keeping the Edge: Managing Defense for the Future,* Cambridge, Mass.: Harvard University Press, 2000.

Casper, Lawrence E., *Falcon Brigade: Combat and Command in Somalia and Haiti,* Boulder, Colo.: Lynne Rienner, 2001.

Cheney, Dick, PBS "Frontline" interview (original airdate), January 9, 1996, available at http://www.pbs.org/wgbh/pages/frontline/gulf/oral/cheney/1.html, accessed May 5, 2001.

Cimbala, Stephen J., "Military Persuasion and the American Way of War," *Strategic Review,* Vol. 22, No. 4 (Fall 1994), pp. 33–43.

_____, *Strategy After Deterrence,* New York: Praeger, 1991.

Clark, Wesley K., *Waging Modern War: Bosnia, Kosovo, and the Future of Combat,* New York: PublicAffairs, 2001.

Clodfelter, Mark, *The Limits of Air Power: The American Bombing of North Vietnam,* New York: The Free Press, 1989.

Coakley, Robert W., *Operation Arkansas,* Washington, D.C.: Histories Division, Office of the Chief of Military History, Department of the Army, 1967.

_____, Paul J. Scheips, and Vincent H. Demma, *Use of Troops in Civil Disturbances Since World War II, 1945–1965,* Washington, D.C.: Office of Military History, U.S. Army, 1971.

Cole, Ronald H., *Operation Just Cause: The Planning and Execution of Joint Operations in Panama, February 1988–January 1990,* Washington, D.C.: Joint History Office, Office of the Chairman of the Joint Chiefs of Staff, 1995.

_____, *Operation Urgent Fury: The Planning and Execution of Joint Operations in Grenada, 12 October–2 November 1983,* Washington, D.C.: Joint History Office, 1997.

Cordesman, Anthony H., and Abraham R. Wagner, *Lessons of Modern War,* Volumes 1–4, Boulder, Colo.: Westview, 1990–1996.

Critchlow, Robert D., "Whom the Gods Would Destroy: An Information Warfare Alternative for Deterrence and Compellence," *Naval War College Review,* Vol. 53, No. 3 (Summer 2000), pp. 21–38.

Darby, Phillip, *British Defence Policy East of Suez, 1947–1968,* London: Oxford University Press, 1973.

Davis, Brian L., *Qaddafi, Terrorism, and the Origins of the U.S. Attack on Libya,* New York: Praeger, 1990.

Davis, Paul K., ed., *New Challenges for Defense Planning: Rethinking How Much Is Enough,* Santa Monica, Calif.: RAND, MR-400-RC, 1994.

Downs, George, "The Rational Deterrence Debate," *World Politics,* Vol. 41, No. 2 (January 1989), pp. 225–237.

Dror, Yehezkel, *Crazy States: A Counterconventional Strategic Problem,* Milwood, N.Y.: Kraus, 1980.

Dumoulin, André, *La France Militaire et l'Afrique—Coopération et Interventions: Un Etat des Lieux,* Brussels: Groupe de Recherche et d'Information sur la Paix et la Sécurité, 1997.

Dupuy, R. Ernest, and Trevor N. Dupuy, *The Encyclopedia of Military History*, New York: Harper & Row, 1986.

Ehrhard, Thomas P., *Making the Connection: An Air Strategy Analysis Framework*, Maxwell AFB, Ala.: Air University Press, 1995.

Ellsberg, Daniel, *The Theory and Practice of Blackmail*, Santa Monica, Calif.: RAND, P-3883, 1959.

Esty, Daniel C., Jack A. Goldstone, Ted Robert Gurr, Barbara Harff, Marc Levy, Geoffrey D. Dabelko, Pamela T. Surko, and Alan N. Unger, *State Failure Task Force Report: Phase II Findings*, McLean, Va.: Science Applications International Corporation, July 31, 1998.

"Excerpts from Iraqi Document on Meeting with U.S. Envoy," *New York Times*, September 23, 1990, p. A19.

Fehrenbach, T. R., *This Kind of War: The Classic Korean War History*, Washington, D.C.: Brassey's, 1998.

Finch, Raymond C., "A Face of Future Battle: Chechen Fighter Shamil Basayev," *Military Review*, Vol. 77, No. 3 (May–June 1997), pp. 33–41.

_____, "Why the Russian Military Failed in Chechnya," *Foreign Military Studies Office Special Study*, No. 98-16, 1998.

Fishel, John T., "Operation Uphold Democracy: Old Principles, New Realities," *Military Review*, Vol. 77, No. 4 (July–August 1997), pp. 22–30.

Flintham, Victor, *Air Wars and Aircraft*, New York: Facts on File, 1990.

Freedman, Lawrence, *The Evolution of Nuclear Strategy*, second edition, New York: St. Martin's Press, 1989.

_____, ed., *Strategic Coercion: Concepts and Cases*, New York: Oxford University Press, 1998.

"From Social Security to Environment, the Candidates' Positions," *New York Times*, November 5, 2001, p. A45.

Fukuyama, Francis, *The End of History and the Last Man,* New York: Avon Books, 1992.

Gaddis, John Lewis, *Strategies of Containment: A Critical Appraisal of Postwar American National Security Policy,* Oxford, UK: Oxford University Press, 1982.

Galeotti, Mark, "Maintaining the *Status Quo*—Riot Control in Moscow," *Jane's Intelligence Review* (June 1991), pp. 264–268.

George, Alexander L., and William E. Simons, eds., *The Limits of Coercive Diplomacy,* second edition, Boulder, Colo.: Westview, 1994.

George, Alexander L., and Richard Smoke, *Deterrence in American Foreign Policy: Theory and Practice,* New York: Columbia University Press, 1974.

Gibbons, William C., *The U.S. Government and the Vietnam War: Executive and Legislative Roles and Relationships. Part IV: July 1965–January 1968,* Princeton, N.J.: Princeton University Press, 1995.

Gordon, Michael R., "Crisis in the Balkans: Russia; Moscow Says Its Envoy Was a Key to Success," *New York Times,* June 4, 1999, p. A22.

_____, "Bush Would Stop U.S. Peacekeeping in Balkan Fights," *New York Times,* October 21, 2001, p. A1.

_____, and Bernard E. Trainor, *The Generals' War,* Boston: Little, Brown, and Company, 1995.

Grau, Lester W., "The Soviet Experience in Afghanistan," *Military Review,* Vol. 75, No. 5 (1995), pp. 16–27.

Gray, Colin S., "Deterrence Resurrected: Revisiting Some Fundamentals," *Parameters* (Summer 1991), pp. 13–21.

Gray, Peter W., "The Myth of Air Control and the Realities of Imperial Policing," *Aerospace Power Journal,* Vol. 15, No. 3 (Fall 2001), pp. 21–31.

Green, Eloisa, "Haiti: Operations Other Than War," *Foreign Military Studies Office Special Study,* No. 94-93, 1997.

Gritton, Eugene C., Paul K. Davis, Randall Steeb, and John Matsumura, *Ground Forces for a Rapidly Deployable Joint Task Force: First-Week Capabilities for Short-Warning Conflicts,* Santa Monica, Calif.: RAND, MR-1152-OSD/A, 2000.

Haass, Richard N., *Intervention: The Use of American Military Force in the Post–Cold War World,* revised edition, Washington, D.C.: Brookings Institution Press, 1999.

_____, PBS "Frontline" interview (original airdate), January 9, 1996, available at http://www.pbs.org/wgbh/pages/frontline/gulf/oral/haass/1.html, accessed May 2, 2001.

Hamilton, Andrew, "Policing Northern Ireland: Current Issues," *Studies in Conflict and Terrorism,* Vol. 18, No. 3 (July–September 1995), pp. 233–242.

Harknett, Richard J., "The Logic of Conventional Deterrence," *Security Studies,* Vol. 4, No. 1 (Autumn 1994), pp. 86–114.

Harvey, John, *Conventional Deterrence and National Security,* Canberra, Australia: RAAF Air Power Studies Centre, 1997.

Hastings, Max, *The Korean War,* New York: Touchstone, 1987.

_____, and Simon Jenkins, *The Battle for the Falklands,* New York: W.W. Norton & Company, 1984.

Heidelberg Institute for International Conflict Research, "KOSIMO," available at http://www.konflikte.de/hiik/frame_en.html, accessed July 2002.

Herr, William E., *Operation Vigilant Warrior: Conventional Deterrence Theory, Doctrine, and Practice,* Maxwell AFB, Ala.: Air University Press, 1997.

Herring, George C., *America's Longest War,* second edition, New York: Knopf, 1986.

Hirsch, John L., and Robert B. Oakley, *Somalia and Operation Restore Hope: Reflections on Peacemaking and Peacekeeping,* Washington, D.C.: U.S. Institute of Peace Press, 1995.

Horowitz, Michael, and Dan Reiter, "When Does Aerial Bombing Work? Quantitative Empirical Tests, 1917–1999," *Journal of Conflict Resolution,* Vol. 45, No. 2 (April 2001), pp. 147–173.

Hosmer, Stephen T., *The Conflict over Kosovo: Why Milosevic Decided to Settle When He Did,* Santa Monica, Calif.: RAND, MR-1351-AF, 2001.

Hudson, James J., "The Role of the California National Guard During the San Francisco General Strike of 1934," *Military Affairs,* Vol. 46, No. 2 (April 1982), pp. 76–83.

Huggins, Peter W., "Airpower and Gradual Escalation: Reconsidering the Conventional Wisdom," master's thesis, School of Advanced Airpower Studies, 2000.

Huggins, William S., "Deterrence After the Cold War: Conventional Arms and the Prevention of War," *Airpower Journal* (Summer 1993), pp. 1–7.

Huntington, Samuel P., *The Clash of Civilizations and the Remaking of World Order,* New York: Simon & Schuster, 1996.

_____, ed., *The Strategic Imperative,* Cambridge, Mass.: Ballinger, 1982.

Huth, Paul K., *Extended Deterrence and the Prevention of War,* New Haven, Conn.: Yale University Press, 1988.

_____, *Standing Your Ground: Territorial Disputes and International Conflict,* Ann Arbor, Mich.: University of Michigan Press, 1996.

_____, and Bruce Russett, "Testing Deterrence Theory: Rigor Makes a Difference," *World Politics,* Vol. 42, No. 4 (July 1990), pp. 469–471.

Jakobsen, Peter Viggo, *Western Use of Coercive Diplomacy After the Cold War,* New York: St. Martin's Press, 1998.

Janis, Irving L. and Leon Mann, *Decision Making,* New York: The Free Press, 1977.

Jervis, Robert, "Deterrence Theory Revisited," *World Politics*, Vol. 31, No. 2 (January 1979), pp. 289–324.

_____, *Perception and Misperception in International Politics*, Princeton, N.J.: Princeton University Press, 1976.

_____, Richard Ned Lebow, and Janice Gross Stein, eds., *Psychology and Deterrence*, Baltimore: Johns Hopkins University Press, 1985.

Johnson, Wray R., "Air Power and Restraint in Small Wars: Marine Corps Aviation in the Second Nicaraguan Campaign," *Aerospace Power Journal*, Vol. 15, No. 3 (Fall 2001), pp. 32–41.

Joint Publications 1: Joint Warfare of the Armed Forces of the United States, Joint Chiefs of Staff, Washington, D.C., 2000.

Joint Publication 1-02: Department of Defense Dictionary of Military and Associated Terms, Joint Chiefs of Staff, Washington, D.C., 2001.

Joint Publication 2-0: Doctrine for Intelligence Support, Joint Chiefs of Staff, Washington, D.C., 2000.

Joint Publication 2-02: National Intelligence Support to Joint Operations, Joint Chiefs of Staff, Washington, D.C., 1998.

Joint Publication 3-0: Doctrine for Joint Operations, Joint Chiefs of Staff, Washington, D.C., 1995.

Joint Publication 3-07: Joint Doctrine for Military Operations Other Than War, Joint Chiefs of Staff, Washington, D.C., 1995.

Joint Publication 5-0: Doctrine for Planning Joint Operations, Joint Chiefs of Staff, Washington, D.C., 1995.

Kaplan, Fred, *The Wizards of Armageddon*, New York: Simon & Schuster, 1983.

Kaplan, Robert D., *The Coming Anarchy: Shattering the Dreams of the Post Cold War*, New York: Vintage Books, 2000.

Khong, Yuen Foong, *Analogies at War*, Princeton, N.J.: Princeton University Press, 1992.

Kirshner, Jonathan, *Currency and Coercion*, Princeton, N.J.: Princeton University Press, 1995.

_____, "The Microfoundations of Economic Sanctions," *Security Studies*, Vol. 6, No. 3 (Spring 1997), pp. 32–64.

Kosnik, Mark E., "The Military Response to Terrorism," *Naval War College Review*, Vol. 53, No. 2 (Spring 2000).

LaPorte, Leon J., and Mary Ann B. Cummings, "Prompt Deterrence: The Army in Kuwait," *Military Review*, Vol. 77, No. 6 (November–December 1997), pp. 39–44.

Larson, Eric V., *Casualties and Consensus*, Santa Monica, Calif.: RAND, MR-726-RC, 1996.

Lebow, Richard Ned, "Windows of Opportunity: Do States Jump Through Them?" *International Security*, Vol. 9, No. 1 (Summer 1984), pp. 147–186.

"Lessons and Conclusions on the Execution of IFOR Operations and Prospects for a Future Combined Security System: The Peace and Stability of Europe After IFOR—A Joint US/Russian Research Project," Foreign Military Studies Office (FMSO) and Center for Military-Strategic Studies (CMSS), 1998, available at http://call.army.mil/call/fmso/fmsopubs/issues/ifor/toc.htm.

Lewy, Guenter, *America in Vietnam*, New York: Oxford University Press, 1978.

Livingston, Neil, "Iraq's Intentional Omission," *Sea Power*, Vol. 34, No. 6 (June 1991), pp. 29–30.

MacKenzie, Lewis, *Peacekeeper: The Road to Sarajevo*, Vancouver: Douglas and McIntyre, 1993.

Mangold, Peter, "Britain and the Defence of Kuwait, 1956–71," *RUSI Journal*, September 1975, pp. 44–48.

Martin, David C., and John Walcott, *Best Laid Plans: The Inside Story of America's War Against Terrorism*, New York: Harper & Row, 1988.

Mearsheimer, John J., *Conventional Deterrence*, Ithaca, N.Y.: Cornell University Press, 1983.

Mendel, William W., "Combat in Cities: The LA Riots and Operation Rio," available at http://call.army.mil/call/fmso/fmsopubs/issues/rio.html, accessed November 15, 2000.

_____, "Operation Rio: Taking Back the Streets," *Military Review*, Vol. 77, No. 3 (May–June 1997), pp. 11–17.

"Message from the CPSU CC Politburo to Members of the CPSU CC and Other Top Party Officials Regarding the Decision to Intervene in Czechoslovakia, August 19, 1968," at "Prague Spring Index of Historical Documents," available at http://library.thinkquest.org/C001155/documents/, accessed April 30, 2001.

Metz, Steven, "Deterring Conflict Short of War," *Strategic Review*, Vol. 22, No. 4 (Fall 1994), pp. 44–51.

Milburn, Thomas W., "What Constitutes Effective Deterrence?" *Journal of Conflict Resolution*, Vol. 3, No. 2 (June 1959), pp. 138–145.

Morgan, Patrick, *Deterrence: A Conceptual Analysis*, Beverly Hills, Calif.: Sage Publications, 1983.

Mueller, John E., "The Search for the 'Breaking Point' in Vietnam: The Statistics of a Deadly Quarrel," *International Studies Quarterly*, Vol. 24 (December 1980), pp. 497–524.

_____, and Karl Mueller, "The Methodology of Mass Destruction: Assessing Threats in the New World Order," *Journal of Strategic Studies*, Vol. 23, No. 1 (March 2000), pp. 163–187.

Mueller, Karl, "The Essence of Coercive Air Power: A Primer for Military Strategists," *Royal Air Force Air Power Review*, Vol. 4, No. 3 (Autumn 2001), pp. 45–56.

_____, "Strategies of Coercion: Denial, Punishment, and the Future of Air Power," *Security Studies*, Vol. 7, No. 3 (Spring 1998), pp. 182–228.

_____, "Strategy, Asymmetric Deterrence, and Accommodation," Ph.D. dissertation, Princeton University, 1991.

Nardulli, Bruce R., Walter L. Perry, Bruce Pirnie, John Gordon IV, and John G. McGinn, *Disjointed War: Military Operations in Kosovo, 1999*, Santa Monica, Calif.: RAND, MR-1406-A, 2002.

North Atlantic Treaty Organization (NATO), "NATO Fact Sheet: NATO's Role in Bosnia and Herzegovina," August 2000, available at http://www.nato.int/docu/facts/2000/role-bih.htm, accessed May 22, 2001.

_____, "NATO Fact Sheet: NATO's Role in Response to the Conflict in Kosovo," available at http://www.nato.int/kosovo/history.htm, accessed May 9, 2001.

O'Hanlon, Michael, "Stopping a North Korean Invasion: Why Defending South Korea Is Easier Than the Pentagon Thinks," *International Security*, Vol. 22, No. 4 (Spring 1998), pp. 135–176.

Oliker, Olga, *Russia's Chechen Wars, 1994–2000: Lessons from Urban Combat*, Santa Monica, Calif.: RAND, MR-1289-A, 2001.

Oswald, Julian, "Conventional Deterrence and Military Diplomacy," *RUSI Journal*, Vol. 138, No. 2 (Spring 1993), pp. 29–30.

Overy, Richard J., *Why the Allies Won*, New York: W. W. Norton and Company, 1995.

Owen, Robert C., ed., *Operation Deliberate Force: A Case Study in Effective Air Campaigning*, Maxwell AFB, Ala.: Air University Press, 1999.

Pape, Robert A., *Bombing to Win: Air Power and Coercion in War*, Ithaca, N.Y.: Cornell University Press, 1996.

_____, "The Air Force Strikes Back: A Reply to Barry Watts and John Warden," *Security Studies*, Vol. 7, No. 2 (Winter 1997/98), pp. 191–214.

Perlez, Jane, "Rumsfeld Seeks to Withdraw American Troops from Sinai," *New York Times*, April 19, 2001.

Quester, George, *Deterrence Before Hiroshima*, New Brunswick, N.J.: Transaction Books, 1986.

Rabasa, Angel, and Peter Chalk, *Colombian Labyrinth*, Santa Monica, Calif.: RAND, MR-1339-AF, 2001.

Reagan, Ronald, "Address to the Nation on Defense and National Security," March 23, 1983, available at http://www.reagan.utexas.edu/resource/speeches/1983/32383d.htm, accessed May 20, 2001.

Rees, David, *Korea: The Limited War*, New York: St. Martin's Press, 1964.

Reiter, Dan, "Exploding the Powder Keg Myth: Preemptive Wars Almost Never Happen," *International Security*, Vol. 20, No. 2 (Fall 1995), pp. 5–34.

Riehm, Peter J. A., "The USS *Harlan County* Affair," *Military Review*, Vol. 77, No. 4 (July–August, 1997), pp. 31–36.

Roberts, Adam, *Nations in Arms*, second edition, London: Macmillan, 1986.

Sawyer, Ralph D., translator, *The Seven Military Classics of Ancient China*, Boulder, Colo.: Westview Press, 1993.

Schelling, Thomas C., *Arms and Influence*, New Haven, Conn.: Yale University Press, 1966.

_____, *Choice and Consequence*, Cambridge, Mass.: Harvard University Press, 1984.

_____, *The Strategy of Conflict*, revised edition, Cambridge, Mass.: Harvard University Press, 1980.

Schubert, Frank N., and Theresa L. Kraus, eds., *The Whirlwind War: The United States Army in Operations Desert Shield and Desert Storm*, Washington, D.C.: U.S. Army Center for Military History, 1995.

Schwartz, Thomas A., "Statement of General Thomas A. Schwartz, Commander in Chief, United Nations Command/Combined Forces Command and Commander, U.S. Forces Korea, Before the Senate Armed Service Committee: March 27, 2001," Washington, D.C.: Senate Armed Service Committee, 2001.

Schweller, Randall, *Deadly Imbalances*, New York: Columbia University Press, 1998.

Shimshoni, Jonathan, *Israel and Conventional Deterrence*, Ithaca, N.Y.: Cornell University Press, 1988.

Shulsky, Abram N., *Deterrence Theory and Chinese Behavior*, Santa Monica, Calif.: RAND, MR-1161-AF, 2000.

Silber, Laura, and Allan Little, *Yugoslavia: Death of a Nation*, New York: TV Books/Penguin USA, 1996.

Singer, J. David, and Melvin Small, "Correlates of War Project: International and Civil War Data, 1816–1992," available at http://www.umich.edu/~cowproj/.

Snyder, Glenn H., *Deterrence and Defense*, Princeton, N.J.: Princeton University Press, 1961.

Stern, Paul C., Robert Axelrod, Robert Jervis, and Roy Radner, eds., *Perspectives on Deterrence*, New York: Oxford University Press, 1989.

Stillion, John, and David T. Orletsky, *Airbase Vulnerability to Conventional Cruise-Missile and Ballistic-Missile Attacks: Technology, Scenarios, and U.S. Air Force Responses*, Santa Monica, Calif.: RAND, MR-1028-AF, 1999.

Sunday Times of London Insight Team, *War in the Falklands: The Full Story*, New York: Harper & Row, 1982.

Tellis, Ashley, Janice L. Bially, Christopher Layne, and Melissa McPherson, *Measuring National Power in the Postindustrial Age*, Santa Monica, Calif.: RAND, MR-1110-A, 2000.

Thies, Wallace J., *When Governments Collide: Coercion and Diplomacy in the Vietnam Conflict, 1964–1968*, Berkeley, Calif.: University of California Press, 1980.

Thomas, Timothy L., "Deterring Information Warfare: A New Strategic Challenge," *Parameters*, Vol. 26, No. 4 (Winter 1996–1997), pp. 81–91.

"Transcript, Condoleezza Rice on Governor George W. Bush's Foreign Policy, October 12, 2000," available at http://www.cfr.org/p/pubs/Rice_10-12-00_Transcript.html, accessed March 15, 2000.

Treverton, Gregory F., *Framing Compellent Strategies*, Santa Monica, Calif.: RAND, MR-1240-OSD, 2000.

Tubbs, James O., *Beyond Gunboat Diplomacy: Forceful Applications of Airpower in Peace Enforcement Operations*, Maxwell AFB, Ala.: Air University Press, 1997.

United Nations, Department of Public Information, "United Nations Protection Force," September 1996, available at http://www.un.org/Depts/dpko/dpko/co_mission/unprof_b.htm, accessed May 22, 2001.

U.S. Army, *FM 100-17: Mobilization, Deployment, Redeployment, Demobilization*, Washington, D.C., 1992, available at http://www.adtdl.army.mil/cgi-bin/atdl.dll/fm/100-17/10017ch1.htm, accessed May 5, 2001.

U.S. Commission on National Security/21st Century, *Seeking a National Strategy: A Concert for Preserving Security and Promoting Freedom*, Washington, D.C., 2000.

U.S. Department of Defense, Office of Net Assessment, "Fact Sheet: What Is Net Assessment?" undated.

U.S. National Defense Panel, *Transforming Defense: National Security in the 21st Century*, Washington, D.C., 1997.

U.S. Navy, Chief of Naval Operations, *The United States Navy in Desert Shield/Desert Storm*, Washington, D.C.: Naval Historical Center, 1991, available at http://www.history.navy.mil/wars/dstorm/, accessed May 24, 2001.

Watman, Kenneth, Dean Wilkening, John Arquilla, and Brian Nichiporuk, *U.S. Regional Deterrence Strategies*, Santa Monica, Calif.: RAND, MR-490-A/AF, 1995.

Watts, Barry D., "Ignoring Reality: Problems of Theory and Evidence in Security Studies," *Security Studies*, Vol. 7, No. 2 (Winter 1997/98), pp. 115–171.

Webster, William H., *The City in Crisis,* Los Angeles: Office of the Special Advisor to the Board of Police Commissioners, 1992.

Wenger, William V., "Lessons From the Los Angeles Riots," *Marine Corps Gazette,* Vol. 77, No. 3 (March 1993), pp. 41–42.

Westermann, Edward B., "The Limits of Soviet Airpower: The Failure of Military Coercion in Afghanistan, 1979–1989," *Journal of Conflict Studies,* Vol. 19, No. 2 (Fall 1999), pp. 39–71.

White House, The, *A National Security Strategy for a New Century,* Washington, D.C., 1999.

Wilkenfeld, Jonathan, and Michael Brecher, "International Crisis Behavior Project: Data Archive," available at http://web.missouri.edu/~polsjjh/ICB/.

Williams, Cindy, ed., *Holding the Line: U.S. Defense Alternative for the Early 21st Century,* Cambridge, Mass.: MIT Press, 2001.

Winnefeld, James A., Preston Niblack, and Dana J. Johnson, *A League of Airmen: U.S. Air Power in the Gulf War,* Santa Monica, Calif.: RAND MR-343-AF, 1994.

Wolf, Barry, *When the Weak Attack the Strong: Failures of Deterrence,* Santa Monica, Calif.: RAND, N-3261-A, 1991.

Wolf, Julie, "The Invasion of Grenada," available at http://www.pbs.org/wgbh/amex/reagan/peopleevents/pande07.html, accessed May 20, 2001.

Wolfowitz, Paul D., "Remarks to the Carnegie Council, June 27, 1990," available at http://www.fas.org/news/skorea/1990/900627-rok-usia.htm, accessed May 2, 2001.

Zimm, Alan D., "Deterrence: Basic Theory, Principles and Implications," *Strategic Review,* Vol. 25, No. 2 (Spring 1997), pp. 42–50.